Growing Up Famous

The Psychological Complexity of Child Celebrities

by

Sophie Bradley

Dear Esteemed Reader,

Thank you immensely for choosing this book to join your collection. We imagine that you've already embarked on an exploration of ideas within these pages, and we couldn't be happier about it!

Now, if you find yourself chuckling, pondering, or even debating with the words in front of you, we'd absolutely love to hear about it. If you can spare a few moments to pen down your thoughts in a review, we would be as delighted as a dictionary on a spelling bee!

An Amazon review would be excellent - but hey, we're far from picky. Whether it's a scribble on the back of a grocery list, a tweet, or even a message in a bottle (though that might take a while to reach us), your feedback is gold.

Writing a review might not be as fun as a spontaneous dance-off, but we promise it'll bring grins to our faces, warmth to our hearts, and incredibly valuable insights to future readers.

With Gratitude,

Bo Bennett, PhD
Publisher
Archieboy Holdings, LLC.

Table of Contents

Growing Up Famous..**1**
The Psychological Complexity of Child Celebrities.................... 1

Introduction...**1**
The World of Child Celebrities 1
The Paradox of Childhood Fame 5
The Psychological Complexity Unveiled 7

Chapter 1: The Correlation Between Fame and Rebellion **11**
Statistics on Celebrity Outbursts................................... 12
Child Celebrities Gone Rogue: Prime Examples 16
The Unforeseen Risks of Early Stardom 18
Understanding the Act of Rebellion in Child Stars.................... 20

Chapter 2: The Pressure Cooker:
Fame's Toll on Development **24**
Developmental Constraints for Child Celebrities 25
Physical Impact of Early Fame 26
Stars Too Soon: The Psychological Impact............................ 30

Chapter 3: Child Stars and Mental Health **33**
How Fame Influences Mental Stability................................ 35
The Implicit Danger: Suppressed Trauma.............................. 36

Chapter 4: Public Outbursts: A Child Star's Silent Cry...........**40**
Comparing Public Outbursts: Celebrities vs Non-celebrities.... 41

Chapter 5: Parental Influence and the Child Celebrity............**46**

Hollywood Parents: Protectors or Profiteers?............ 47

The Role of Parents in Celebrity Outbursts 50

Helicopter vs. Free-Range: The Best Parenting
Style for Child Stars 53

Chapter 6: Fame, Power, and Abuse in Hollywood **57**

The Unpleasant Side of Stardom: Abuse Stories 57

Power Play: How Systemic Abuse Affects Child Celebrities..... 61

A Rise in Activism and Awareness 64

Chapter 7: Psychological Support for Child Stars **66**

The Importance of a Support System............ 67

Celebrity Stories: The Role of Therapy in Redemption 70

**Chapter 8: The Transition From Child Star to
Adult Celebrity** **74**

Growing Up In the Public Eye: The Trials 75

Coping Mechanism: Building a Healthy Adult
Celebrity Life 77

Rebranding: A Crucial Step for Long Term Success............ 80

Conclusion............**84**

Reflecting on the Celebrity World 84

Introduction

Imagine being stuck in a perpetual childhood, where the rules are contradictory, expectations like monstrous shadows, and your every action scrutinized under a magnifying glass of fame. Welcome to the world of young celebrities, where the gold of public admiration often conceals the flaws inherent in the system. The psychological complexity of early fame can twist the cognitive and emotional development of these children, sometimes resulting in public outbursts that can be as mystifying as they are concerning. This book aims to explore these intricate psychological patterns, delving deep into the minds of child celebrities to understand the impact of fame on their normal psychological upbringing. We'll journey through the paradoxical world of childhood fame, shedding light on not just the shine and glamor but also the emotional stress and strain that is often hidden behind the bright studio lights. In the following chapters, we'll delve into the hidden stories, the silent cries, the mental strains, and ultimately, what can be done to provide a safety net to these young stars. So, let's embark on this exploration, not just with a sense of curiosity, but also of empathy for what being 'famous' can mean when you're still just a kid.

The World of Child Celebrities

Child celebrities. They're adored, they're idolized, and at times even worshipped. Their faces welcomed in millions of homes through the screen, a life most of us only get to see through a filter of glitz and glamour. But beneath the bright lights and maelstrom of camera flashes exists a world that is less understood, less friendly, and shockingly more complex.

Children thrown into the fierce realm of fame before their adolescence face unique challenges. They are expected to shed their innocent childhood and grow up in an impossibly short amount of time, handling not only their own development but also the expectations and gaze of an often judgmental public.

From the outside looking in, it appears all shiny and glittered up—red carpets, instant recognition, unending gifts and vast wealth, parties, and contacts with big-shots. The world of child stars can seem like the 'Alice in Wonderland' most kids dream of inhabiting. But is it really the wonderland it appears to be?

As you delve deeper, it becomes increasingly clear that fame and fortune come with a hefty price. The experience can overwhelm, leading not to infamy as one might expect, but rather to a complex psychological landscape less travelled by average adolescents. Life in the limelight does add a level of sophistication, but it can also cast dark shadows on the young and impressionable minds dealing with the unique stressors of fame.

Child celebrities are not only acting on a script, they are also expected to act as role models for their fans. They are put on pedestals and are expected to behave a certain way - mature, composed, and sophisticated well before they've had a chance to be just regular kids. Their actions and behaviors are scrutinized heavily, to a point where they can feel trapped under the weight of fame.

The paradox of childhood fame is that it offers a taste of power, visibility, and significance, yet simultaneously removes the child's ability to shape their identity out of the public spotlight. The glare of incessant attention can sometimes be bright enough to blur the line between the characters they play on screen and their own selves.

Such oversized expectations can build up a colossal pressure – a pressure that not only affects the course of a child's normal development, but gradually gnaws away at their resilience, leaving them grappling with effects of early fame. The playgrounds are traded for studios, the toys for awards, and the classmates for fans and followers. It's a life atypical, different from any we understand, a life that only a child star knows.

For every child actor who successfully makes the transition to adulthood, remaining in control of their lives and careers, there are numerous others who haven't fared so well. The stark, stark contrast between their real life and reel life often leads to confusion, anxiety, depression, and in severe cases, damage beyond repair.

Celebrity outbursts aren't uncommon. After all, they're humans too, subjected to the same emotional turmoil that any of us face. However, for young celebrities, these incidents can be a manifestation of their struggle, their silent cry for help, their rebellion against a world that expects too much too soon.

The role of parents in young stars' lives is pivotal, walking the fine line between crucial support and unwitting exploitation. The world has seen both types, those who act as strong buffers, guiding their child through the complexities of fame, and then there are others whose thirst for personal gain leads them to conveniently overlook their child's needs and vulnerabilities.

The darker side of stardom isn't just about the fame-induced stress, it's also about the power dynamics within the industry. It's an unpleasant truth, but the industry has had its fair share of people misusing their influence, leading to distressing cases of exploitation and harassment of young, impressionable celebrities.

The good news though is that the industry is changing. There's been increasing awareness and activism against such exploitation and increasing support networks for young artists. Therapy is becoming more widely accepted as a strategy for brightening their future paths.

Each child star's journey through fame, through the complicated maze of stardom is unique. Some continue to shine, learning to live with the pressures of fame and making it a part of their identity. Some implode under the pressure, while others, void-fill their lives with substance abuse and scandals.

Ultimately, child stardom is a complex realm of contradictory experiences: a collision of fame, childhood, power, and vulnerability. The world of child celebrities, it's as enchanting as it is bewildering and as promising as it is perilous.

From Innocence to Infamy ... When we first meet these young talents, there's a sense of gleaming innocence that draws us in. Pint-sized prodigies with potential overflowing, they enter the limelight—carrying hopes of entertaining millions and dreams of lifelong glamor. Their smiles are bright and eyes filled with wonder as they innocently navigate through a world far from their local kindergarten playground.

Yet a swift dance later, this gleam turns into a stormy gaze. Faced with an onslaught of expectations from fans, demands from producers, and pressure from the media, these youngsters are thrust into the vicious cycle of fame. This often premature and unprepared foray into the limelight can radically alter their path—from those early days of innocence to a spiraling journey towards infamy. The physical demands, social activities, and emotional struggles they face can quickly outweigh the glittery appeal of fame and transform these fresh-faced child stars into adolescents grappling with public outbursts and rebellion.

Then comes the hidden repercussions—trailing not far behind the stardom are emotional tug-of-war, identity crises, and impaired social skills. The childhood that's replaced by adult-like responsibilities and public scrutiny can stagnate their developmental growth. This abrupt shift from playing with toys to confronting paparazzi and tabloids can often lead these budding personalities towards the path of infamy, tarnishing their innocence. The solitary life that accompanies fame, the intense scrutiny, and the harsh criticism levelled at these young minds fosters a fertile ground for rebellion. In this section, we will delve deeper into this relatively unseen transition from innocence to infamy among child celebrities and its accompanying turmoil and tribulations.

The Paradox of Childhood Fame

After adding a little bit of context about the world of child celebrities and their transition from innocence to infamy, it's now time to dig deeper into our discussion- into the paradox of childhood fame. While fame at an early age often signifies incredible talent and a promising future, it's also a twisting double-edged sword that can lead to complications in a child's personal and professional life.

Recognizing these struggles, society often labels the journey of a child star as "living a dream". Now, that's where we come across an irony—a contradiction if you will. On the one hand, these children are adored by multitudes and have access to opportunities that may seem far-fetched for many. From jet-setting to appearances on red carpets and luxury at their fingertips— it almost seems like a fairy tale. But hold onto that thought for a moment.

Contrarily, being a child star, at times, means surrendering aspects of conventional and healthy child development imperative for one's psychological wellbeing. This surrender can lead to severe emotional stress and difficulty in discerning real affection from superficial attention. Suddenly, the not-so-glamorous picture behind the scenes doesn't seem as rosy, right?

Moreover, the continuous scrutinization under the public eye can lead to an immense pressure to maintain a particular image or persona. This false image, while often facilitated by managers or industry standards, can pave the way to identity crises and instability in later years. It's as if these celebrities are lost to find their true selves while creating an unreal image for the world.

While the casual observer might not discern this paradox, it's increasingly obvious to those who have a closer view. The dilemma therein lies in the seemingly harmless spotlight stealing away invaluable experiences that constitute a "normal" childhood. This is particularly problematic as the loss often remains unnoticed until the adverse effects start to surface in adolescence, or even in their adulthood.

Not to mention, the world of fame and fortune might attract predators ready to exploit the innocent for their personal gain. The child is thrown into situations beyond their capacity to comprehend, or cope with, creating hurdles in their emotional and psychological growth. The show must go on, they say.

Furthermore, the paradox continues as childhood fame can create unrealistic expectations for future success. With their talent peaking at such an early age, they are burdened with fears of what if everything just goes downhill from there. It's quite the paradox indeed—a childhood full of accomplishments yet haunted by fear of fading away.

The double-edged sword, the roller coaster ride, the Paradox—call it what you may. The overarching theme remains the same. Caught between the complex interplay of innocence and fame, these child celebrities step into a world that far exceeds their tender years. Regardless of the tempting glamour and the appeal it may exude, living in the spotlight has its price—a cost often camouflaged by glitz, with repercussions that seldom make it to the headlines.

Stay with us as we delve deeper to uncover the complexities that entangle the minds of young stars and continue on this journey into the world of childhood fame.

Where the Sidewalk Ends: The Childhood Fame Lane begins where every child's journey into stardom must – at the very edge of innocence, where normalcy and fame intersect. The journey for a child star can be seen as a lane that leads away from the wide, safe sidewalks of a typical childhood. Instead, their path is lined with the bright and glaring lights of the paparazzi, filled with the echoing cheers of adoring fans. They move at double speed, trading playgrounds for movie sets and homework for scripts, events that morph their carefree world into an unpredictable roller coaster of emotions.

Just as fame presents its fair share of sparkling gems – the money, recognition, and access – it also introduces these young stars to challenges that are quite foreign to their peers. One moment they're playing make-believe with their friends, and the next they are pretending for real in front of thousands. Navigating this space can be a challenge and a half. It's a heavy crown to bear, as they transform into their character on cue while real personal development is quietly pushed to the backdrop eating away at their innocent childhood.

And so, they find themselves on the dreaded childhood fame lane, where life's lessons are learned at a price and magnified for all to see. They're expected to be models of perfection, grace, and talent, while simultaneously navigating the turbulent waters of adolescence. They're often held to an impossible standard, one where mistakes are not allowed, and any stumble could potentially be fatal to their careers. It's a high-pressure environment that can intensify emotions and nudge them towards public outbursts. While these circumstances may sound daunting, they're unfortunately the reality for many young celebs. The next section will dive deeper into this complexity of their unique psychological makeup, shedding more light on how they manage to juggle fame and normalcy.

The Psychological Complexity Unveiled

The public might perceive child stars as glorified mini adults who sail through life on a wave of applause and accolades. But hidden beneath this facade lies a complex psychological tapestry. These young stars may have tens of thousands of followers on social media, yes, but they also have tens of thousands of opinions aimed directly at them, tinged with expectations and scrutiny few regular children encounter.

For some, climbing the glittering heights of fame is a dream come true. But neither the audience nor the stars themselves are often aware of the possible fall. And when that fall happens, it is rarely glamorous. The psychological complexity of these youngsters remains veiled beneath the red carpet walk and award-winning smiles.

Fame is a complex beast that demands an equally complex sacrifice; the psychological development and normative growth of these child stars. By thrusting them into limelight long before their minds and emotional maturity are ready, we're indirectly hammering on their cognitive development. The maddening pace of being in showbiz can stunt their emotional growth, creating a flawed foundation that further endangers their mental state.

Imagine entering a world where privacy is a myth, the lines between real and fake blur, and judgement and opinions are tossed around like confetti. It's a world that can shake the confidence of even the most seasoned adults, let alone children. This constant scrutiny can cloud their self-perception and beliefs, affecting their development of a stable identity.

Many of these youngsters move through their fame-infused lives feeling misplaced. Unlike their non-famous counterparts, they find themselves navigating adult dynamics and power plays sooner than their psychological growth can handle. Too soon, they are juggling fame and identity, success and failure, public image and private self, adulation and criticism.

Take a moment to think about the delicacy of the adolescent mind. Now, add into that the pressure of constantly being in the public eye, and we start to unveil the psychosocial cost of precocious fame. The world starts to make demands of them, wanting them to be precociously mature in performing their skills, yet immature and untouched by the ways of the adult world.

These divergent pressures can lead child stars towards rebellious behaviors, public outbursts, and excessive substance use. We often view these as pointless acts of deviance. Still, in reality, they may be efforts to claim a sense of agency or self-determination, to carve out a semblance of normalcy amid the abnormal.

As the wall between the self and the public image erodes, these youngsters may begin to internalize the celebrity persona until they can hardly distinguish their authentic selves. This erosion can lead to a reality where their self-construct becomes dependent on external validation and feedback, rather than being rooted in personal values and healthy self-esteem.

As we delve deeper into the minds of these young stars, it becomes clear that fame is an enticing but a double-edged sword. The glitz and glamour of the entertainment world often overshadow the mental and emotional cost that these young celebrities have to bear. It asserts the need to peel back the curtain on this complex issue and find ways to nurture these bright minds, ensuring that the starlight doesn't succumb to shadow.

The psychological complexity of child celebrities, therefore, is a reality that needs to be acknowledged, understood, and addressed. It's crucial to remember that beneath the spotlight, they are just children, burdened with the complexities of fame before they can fully comprehend the nuances of their rapidly changing world.

A Peek into the Minds of Young Stars Being a child star can feel like walking on a tightrope. On one side, there's the dazzling allure of stardom, a world filled with glittering praise, ceaseless attention, and luxurious amenities. On the other side, there's a void filled with anxiety, the pressure of performance, and the haunting fear of failure. It's a balancing act, teetering between the sky-high expectations and the equally bottomless reality of those expectations not being met.

The public, enamoured by the glitz, often overlooks the psychological vulnerability of these stars. Exposure to harsh public scrutiny at a tender age can leave an indelible mark on their psyche. They're expected to perform to perfection, and even the slightest misstep can get magnified under the spotlight. Imagine being under a constant watch, every action dissected and evaluated. That's a tremendous load for young shoulders.

Now consider the dichotomy of their personal and professional life. Young stars try to juggle their schoolwork, soccer practice, and play dates with their friends, all while undertaking screen tests, memorizing lines, and performing in front of camera crews. This unorthodox routine, vastly different from a 'normal' child's life, might sometimes lead to feelings of isolation, questioning their identity, and even resentment for being 'different'.

Apart from the psychological burden, these stars ceaselessly grapple with the fear of obscurity. Their status is often ephemeral, leading to a constant struggle to remain relevant and in the limelight. This could, subsequently, trigger the fear of rejection, compounding the emotional stress. Such constant pressures can make maintaining a sense of self particularly challenging, often leading to tumultuous emotional eruptions.

It is no wonder then, that in trying to reconcile their stardom with their own identity, these young stars may frequently display erratic behavior. Public outbursts, brushes with law enforcement, or drastic changes in appearance may be coping mechanisms or cries for help hidden behind the flare of sensationalized headlines. It's important to empathize, to understand the world they navigate is vastly more complicated than meets the eye. Truly, a introspection into the minds of these young stars reveals a complex terrain filled with trials and tribulations.

Chapter 1:
The Correlation Between Fame and Rebellion

At face value, the juxtaposition of a child star's innocent glow and the flamed charisma of rebellion seems startling, even unnatural. But in reality, it's a gripping spectacle that we've seen uncurl far too often due to the high-profile nature of fame paired with an alluring taste for exploration commonly found in youth. So, what exactly entices these young luminaries to deviate from the well-trodden path of quintessential teenage milestones? The correlation between fame and rebellion lies, fundamentally, in the unique social and psychological pressures that these children experience. Their lives are often a far cry from normalcy, filled with high-intensity performances, public scrutiny, and a relentless pursuit of success. As a sort of countermovement, rebellion offers an escape route, a way to exert control over their personal narrative in a life that is often painstakingly choreographed. This whirlwind, under the magnifying glass of stardom, compounds the impact of each rebellious act, escalating what would be normal adolescent indiscretions into headline-grabbing outbursts. The challenge then becomes discerning acts of rebellion that are natural components of growing up from those pathological expressions of stress under the limelight, a task made even more complex by the publicity machine that fuels their fame. The end goal is a balance, a symbiosis if you will, that allow these young stars to experience the freedoms and mistakes of youth without capitulating to a life of chaos and ruin.

Statistics on Celebrity Outbursts

When it comes to fame, one phenomenon that seems to be prevalent, particularly in the world of child stars, is the occurrence of public outbursts. While it's not exclusive to the realm of the famous, it certainly seems to be accentuated due to the constant spotlight and the high-pressure environments that these young stars inhabit.

The statistics don't lie: celebrity outbursts unsurprisingly outnumber those of non-famous adolescents. It's a stark reminder that despite the glitz, fame, and fortune, child stars aren't immune to the pressures and difficulties young people encounter throughout their adolescence. In some cases, the fame intensifies these challenges, catalyzing public behavioral explosions quite regularly.

However, the numbers do more than simply count the instances of these unfortunate episodes; they also present some insights about the reasons for such explosions. Digging deeper, we notice a disturbing pattern: child stars often live in a world of relentless stress, rigorous schedules, and extreme public scrutiny. Not exactly an ideal environment to navigate through the tumultuous years of adolescence.

According to several studies, child celebrities are known to commence therapy or counseling significantly earlier than their non-famous counterparts, indicating that struggles with mental health are a common thread among them. These professional interventions often come about as an aftermath of some form of public outburst, revealing the volatile ambiance of this microcosm.

A report from the American Psychological Association (APA) shed some light on this situation. It highlighted that 24% of child stars had reported severe depression, compared to only 13% of ordinary adolescents. Other mental health issues, like anxiety disorders and substance abuse, were also found to be higher amongst young celebrities.

The report, furthermore, displayed a telling correlation: the pressure that child stars experienced significantly influenced their likeliness to display volatile behavior in the form of public disturbances. Such incidents rose in tandem with heightened stress, fast-paced work environments, and lack of personal privacy.

Moreover, a sizable fraction of these individuals has entanglements with the law, way more than the children outside the showbiz perimeter. This is an alarming realization that goes beyond mere numbers, suggesting the manifestation of deeper psychological issues in this vulnerable group.

In fact, the juvenile justice system's statistics have shown that arrested child celebrities often had double the rate of recidivism amongst the delinquent population. This indicates a strained relationship between the child stars and the societal laws, causing them to repeatedly clash with authority, contributing to their infamous outbursts.

On a similar vein, statistics relating to academic performance have shown a distinct trend amongst child stars who aren't subjected to proper institutional schooling. It was noticed that their academic abilities were generally inferior compared to those who attended traditional schools. It's a pivotal point, for education deprivation can lead to stunted social development, fostering feelings of resentment and frustration, which potentially could be channeled into public outbursts.

Perhaps the most compelling statistic involves the lifespan of these child stars. A 2012 study published in the Journal of Epidemiology and Community Health found that child stars tend to have a shorter average life expectancy compared to those in other occupations. This grim revelation serves as a morbid testament to the pressure the fame-infused environment can place on young shoulders, leaving them vulnerable, prone to outbursts, and sometimes leading to premature death.

In conclusion, the statistics reveal the stark reality and multi-faceted influences behind the public outbursts seen amongst child stars. It's a complex mesh of emotional, psychological, and societal factors coalescing under the unforgiving spotlight. It's about understanding that these cases aren't isolated incidents but rather symptomatic responses to an often ruthless reality masked behind the coveted Hollywood sign.

Furthermore, it sheds light on the urgent need for protective measures to alleviate the pressures from these young celebrities and guidance to develop robust coping mechanisms. Wouldn't it be better if the statistics would tell a story of successful transition, resilience and maturing well under pressure instead?

As we delve further into the correlation between fame and rebellion, this statistical foundation will underpin our attempt to fully understand the landscape these child celebrities navigate. Every statistic tells a story, and to fully grasp the depth of this situation, we must listen closely to every tale they tell.

A Comparison with Non-Famed Adolescents creates an interesting perspective, shedding light on the distinction in behavioural patterns between child celebrities and those growing up in non-public scenarios. It's no secret celebrities live a life that's far from ordinary, further complicated when fame knocks on their door at such a tender age.

Fame brings with it constant scrutiny, amplified expectation and an unasked for level of responsibility, a stark contrast to the more ordinary experiences of a non-famed adolescent. Let's consider, for a moment, a typical teenager. They are on a journey of self-discovery, figuring out their identity, pursuing interests and grappling with school stressors, family dynamics, peer pressure and awkward growth spurts. The teenage years are designed for mistakes, adventures, heartbreaks and lessons, all relatively shielded from the judgemental public eye.

Contrast this to child celebrities, where each moment, each action reverberates nationally or even globally. For them, errors in judgement or behavioral missteps quickly escalate into tabloid headlines, provoking both public shame and ridicule. A phase that should be private and forgiving is instead lived out before millions. This dynamic naturally magnifies the repercussions of typical teenage rebellion and antics.

Moreover, consider the level of independence and decision-making power that a typical adolescent enjoys. They have the freedom to choose, to try, to fail and to learn. However, in the high-stakes world of fame, child stars often lack this luxury. The industry's pressures influence them and the decisions they make, limiting their capacity to independently explore their identity.

For a standard teen, rebellion might mean coming home past curfew, experimenting with fashion choices, or arguing about chores. This rebellion, pivotal for self-discovery and boundary setting, plays out quietly within the privacy of homes and schools.

Now, when a child star rebels, it can take on an entirely different magnitude compared to their non-famed counterparts. Their rebellion often ends up in headlines, making them fodder for gossip and public judgement. Whether it's a scandalous tweet, a controversial outfit or a run-in with the law, these lapses highlight the intensity with which every action of theirs is scrutinized and criticized.

A stark comparison also lies in the avenues of social interaction for both sets. A non-famed teen's social interactions are primarily in school, sports teams or neighborhood friends where they learn to navigate relationships, face rejection and build resilience. Child celebrities, bound by their schedules and constant supervision, find their interaction environments limited. This restriction can lead to isolation, thereby depriving them of necessary social skills.

Another aspect worth noting is the access to resources. Typical teenagers might get part-time jobs, managing their budget and experiencing the value of hard work firsthand. Child celebrities, with finances often managed by other parties, may miss out on this grounding experience. This can sometimes create a false sense of entitlement and disconnect with reality.

Now, this isn't to say that every child celebrity falls victim to the pitfalls of early fame. Several navigate the same successfully. But the underlying comparison underscores the challenges that child stars face owing to their fame, and the strength and resilience required to not let it overwhelm their adolescence.

To conclude, the difference in the treaded paths of child celebrities and non-famed adolescents is quite pronounced. Recognizing these disparities and the complex implications they have on the psychology of young stars is key to understanding, empathizing, and supporting them in their unique struggle.

Child Celebrities Gone Rogue: Prime Examples

Continuing our exploration of the correlation between fame and rebellion, we step into the arena of specific cases. After all, it's through real-world examples that we can best witness the impact of childhood stardom. They paint a realistic, if not always pretty, picture of the volatile mix of fame and youth.

We kick things off with the infamous case of a gifted child actor who initially won hearts with zesty performances. As he aged, what we witnessed was disconcerting. A string of legal issues, substance abuse and seemingly unprovoked aggressive behavior made headlines far too often. It was a painful reminder of how, despite all the fame and fortune, child stars are not immune to the pitfalls of adolescence. While the world watched these unruly episodes unfold, it was clear this was not just a classic teenage rebellion; fame had a role, too.

Next, we move to a young actress who transitioned from a lovable sitcom character to hardcore partygoer. The image transformation was drastic and reflected a yearning for autonomy. Yes, she was pursuing adult roles, but the shift was also a direct push against societal expectations. When a child star violates the innocent image that audiences have come to adore, it's an act of rebellion. Sadly, her mental health suffered in the process.

A teen heartthrob gone wild serves as an excellent example of the price one pays for early fame. There's no discounting his talent or phenomenal success, but underneath the shining exterior was a boy struggling to keep his footing in the adult world. The infractions of law, the physical altercations, all showed a desire to break away from the docile, pre-packaged image served to his fans.

Let's not forget the child singer who, after years of carefully managed appearances and catchy singles, went through a tumultuous phase. This episode contained a multitude of drastic image makeovers, onstage outbursts, and a fair share of headline-making antics. Deeper down, it was a quest for individuality, one that was amplified by the boa-constrictor grip of fame.

Then, there is the case of the famous twins, who grew up in front of the camera, playing adorable toddlers first and later teens. When they opted for semi-retirement from acting well before their twenties, the world gasped. One of them made a shocking admission about their struggle with an eating disorder. Their withdrawal from acting was an assertion of their need for privacy, thereby rebelling against the intrusive nature of fame.

Let's not leave out the bright actor whose performances in family-friendly films endeared him to audiences. His unruly behavior, both on and off-set, however, painted a dissonant picture. Rather than growing up, it seemed he was acting out, wrestling with the invisible chains of his childhood fame.

Finally, an adolescent band member turned solo artist found herself headlining tabloids for her intoxicating lifestyle rather than her chart-topping hits. It was disquieting to see how, despite her musical success, she was battling substance abuse and dealing with tumultuous relationships. It served as a stark reminder that fame, when conflated with the already volatile period of adolescence, can breed disaster.

These stories illustrate the tumultuous journey of child celebrities grappling with fame and recognizing their autonomy. It's clear that these kids didn't just wake up one day deciding to go rogue. Their rebellious actions often stemmed from an underlying psychological struggle: a desperate need for normalcy tugging against the intense pressure of fame.

Yet, it's crucial to remember that these examples are not indicative of every child star's journey. Not all child celebrities match these cautionary tales. There are many who tread through the storm of adolescence with grace and emerge stronger despite the magnifying lens of fame.

What proves consistent, however, is the unique challenges these young stars face. Armed with these tales, we must now delve deeper into why such rebelliousness arises in child stars. In understanding the roots, it's possible to foster better support systems for these young talents caught between the allure of stardom and the challenges of youth.

The Unforeseen Risks of Early Stardom

When we unpack the lives of these youngsters, we witness the cruel irony that accompanies their fame. The rewards of celebrity often counteract the unpredictable undercurrents these youth must navigate. On the glossy surface, they have success and recognition that many covet, but beneath, they grapple with identity crises, mental health issues, and even exploitation.

We now transition into examining the unseen risks that lurk in the shadows of early stardom. How do these factors feed into the rebellious behaviors we've discussed? More importantly, how can we mitigate these risks to ensure a healthier trajectory for the young stars of today and tomorrow? Offering an inside look into these concerns opens the door to creating a more supportive entertainment industry.

The Unforeseen Risks of Early Stardom While fame is usually portrayed as glitz and glamour, the reality for child celebrities often deviates heavily from this idealistic vision. Early stardom carries a burdensome weight representing both dreams achieved and the startling reality of a life permanently altered. For these youngsters, navigating stardom can be fraught with unforeseen risks, that can, ironically, dim the glamour poured on them as they set foot on the red-carpeted avenues of fame.

First off, for a very young star, the instant fame can create an overwhelming burden. This happens as their identities are still congealing. It's like they're caught in this whirlwind of public interest and suddenly, they've got a brand to manage and an image to uphold. Can you imagine the strain that places on a young adolescent's developing psyche? Their emotional growth can flat-out stagnate amid star-studded, overwhelming conditions that include an expectation for perfection, a necessity to sustain public adoration and a pressure to constantly perform, both on-screen and off.

Secondly, the magnitude of their stardom sometimes makes them targets for unscrupulous folks aiming to exploit their fame for personal gain. They are liable to fall prey to manipulative authorities, opportunistic friends, and hangers-on. Even parents and family can become entwined in the lure of fame and fortune, forgetting the susceptible, still-maturing individual amidst the glitz and the glamour. The risk of such exploitation is a grim, yet very real aspect of child stardom, and it can initiate a sentiment of mistrust and skepticism that can haunt their relationships for years to come.

Unhealthy coping mechanisms often rear their ugly heads as a byproduct of this environment. When overwhelmed with the pressures of fame, some child stars resort to substance abuse, eating disorders, or other destructive habits as a means of escape. The resulting mental health issues, such as anxiety or depression, can persist into adulthood, serving as a constant reminder of a stolen childhood and casting a haunting shadow over their lives.

Finally, early stardom often leads to trouble transitioning into a regular childhood or adolescence. Without limits on work hours and those normal school experiences to ground them, child celebrities can feel adrift in a sea of adult expectations and demands. They miss out on the everyday experiences that piece together a typical childhood or teenage life, and once their star fades, the return to a semblance of a normal life becomes an herculean task. For these child stars, it's about living backward; from adult-like responsibilities towards the yearning for a chance to grow up, a chance they feel was cruelly stolen from them.

Understanding the Act of Rebellion in Child Stars

Rebellion in child stars often strikes a chord with the public. It's a topic that generates much interest, as we grapple to understand the behavioral patterns of these young celebrities undergoing the tricky metamorphosis from endearing child star to adult icon. This rebellion isn't merely an act of errant conduct or due to immaturity; it emanates from complex layers of psychological strife that are peculiar to the stardom that these kids are thrust into.

The psychological canvas of child stars is unique. They live a paradoxical existence—enjoying colossal fame and fortune but simultaneously missing out on aspects of regular childhood. It's crucial to realize that these early brushes with fame come with immense consequences. Stardom doesn't merely influence their lifestyle choices; it significantly impacts their perceptions about life, relationships, and themselves.

Rebellion observed in child stars generally includes wild partying, substance abuse, legal troubles, and public outbursts. However, these actions often are surface symptoms of a much deeper psychological struggle, often linked with their early exposure to fame. The rebellions aren't mere missteps; they're expressions of deeper conflicts and bottled-up frustrations.

Research on adolescent development indicates that teenagers push boundaries as part of their cognitive and emotional growth. However, for child stars, this natural element of development heavily magnifies due to their lives' public nature and the high stakes associated with their image. Their actions are continually scrutinized, judged, and often, blown out of proportion, resulting in additional stress and pressure, exacerbating the rebellious behavior.

One core factor fueling rebellion in child stars is the tug-of-war between their public persona and their real selves. The expectation to conform to a specific image or character can be considerably suffocating. Many child celebrities want to break free from this image trap, expressing themselves authentically, even if it goes against the public's approval.

Further, the rebellion sometimes is a desperate plea for normalcy. Surrounded by a sea of adult pressures and expectations, these child stars long for normal childhood experiences. The stringent schedules, promotional commitments, and heightened expectations rob them of their playtime, friendships, and typical adolescent experiences. This deprivation often causes resentment, leading to acts of rebellion.

Also, child stars frequently need to deal with tumultuous relationships, a result of grown-up issues like contractual disputes, competition, and image management. Rebellion can be a way for them to communicate their distress or to gain power in their complicated lives where they often feel powerless.

The early exposure to fame also tends to create a void in their personalities due to the excessive external validation. Once this validation diminishes, they may struggle with their self-worth, giving rise to feelings of insecurity, anger, or resentment. Rebellion, in these instances, can be an attempt to regain relevance and public attention.

Lastly, a lack of an effective support system often fails to guide child stars in responsibly handling their fame, wealth, and public image. Unregulated freedom coupled with massive spending power can result in reckless behaviors and decisions.

Understanding this act of rebellion in child stars is vital for addressing the core challenges they face. Ultimately, focused and consistent support from parents, industry professionals, and mental health experts can significantly help these young talents navigate their tumultuous journey through childhood fame, mitigating the potential for rebellious behavior.

The Tug-of-War Between Normalcy and Stardom often emerges as an essential part of the narrative when discussing child celebrities. When a child is thrust into the spotlight at a young age, they are usually forced to grapple with an imbalance in their life. On one hand, they're expected to maintain what society defines as a normal childhood - going to school, making friends and participating in quintessential adolescent activities. On the other, they are faced with the high-pressure, high-stakes world of Hollywood, replete with spotlights, adoring fans and, sometimes, harsh critics. It's a balancing act; a delicate dance between the ordinary and the extraordinary.

However, this tug-of-war comes with pitfalls. Children are still forming their identities, still figuring out who they are and who they want to be. Now imagine adding fame to the mix. They've got to handle their character under scrutiny in the public eye, the relentless pursuit by paparazzi, and the perniciously double-edged sword of social media. The pressure is enough to sway even the most grounded individuals, let alone a child. It can lead to a sense of disillusionment, a skewed perception of self-worth, and an unfortunate susceptibility to questionable influences.

Moreover, this struggle between normalcy and stardom can fuel the act of rebellion, as observed in numerous instances. It's not about being naughty or disobedient for the sake of it. But rather, it is an outcry for normalcy, in an attempt to reclaim the childhood that has been snatched away from them by fame. At the end of the day, these are just kids trying to find their footing in a world that's made them larger than life. It's essential to realize that behind every headline-worthy outburst, there's a tug-of-war between a normal child and the star that they are expected to be.

Chapter 2:
The Pressure Cooker:
Fame's Toll on Development

If you thought growing up was tough, imagine it under the glare of spotlights with every misstep dissected by the public. A peculiar blend of external pressures and increased expectations characterizes the life of a child celebrity, akin to living in a pressure cooker of fame where typical growth patterns are disrupted. They're trading playground adventures for the whirlwind limelight, a change that often stunts critical facets of their developmental journey. Often, these development impediments manifest physically due to the stress of managing a public persona, affecting not just their emotional equilibrium but also their physical well-being. While the dazzle of fame might seem alluring, the stars too young bear a psychological burden unlike anything faced by non-famed kids. Their world isn't as simple as school and play; instead, it spirals into a complex labyrinth of public expectations, professional commitments and a desperate struggle for normalcy. The cost of fame isn't just measured in paparazzi ambushes or lack of privacy; it's a gravely serious spectrum of psychological stress that relentlessly chips away at the young mind, mounting a weight that far outweighs their years. As we navigate through this chapter, we will delve deeper into the developmental constraints placed on child stars, understand the physical and psychological impacts of early fame, and why sometimes, all that glitters isn't gold.

Developmental Constraints for Child Celebrities

A primary challenge for child celebrities is growing up within the bounds of normalcy. Often, they are shuttled from one set to another, their days crammed with interviews, shoots, dancing, acting, singing, or modeling rehearsals. As fascinating and thrilling as this lifestyle might sound to the onlooker, it inhibits children's natural development in a myriad of ways.

Instead of participating in regular schools, most young stars attend on-set tutoring sessions where the focus usually lies more on completing the state-mandated education requirements rather than providing an enriching learning environment. They're unlikely to experience the innocent yet crucial events that most kids their age do, such as building friendships, experiencing crushes, playing for sports teams, or even grappling with petty schoolyard squabbles. Missed out on these are foundational social-skills-learning opportunities that are essential to natural development.

Children are naturally curious creatures, buzzing with energy, passion, questions, and a thirst for knowledge. In a standard upbringing, children are allowed to explore this curiosity freely, ask endless questions, learn organically, and develop at their own pace, making mistakes and learning from them. The world, to them, is a playground for exploration and learning.

Unfortunately, child stars often don't have this luxury. Their lives are meticulously planned and stage-managed, with scarcely any room for organic exploration or self-driven learning. This regimented lifestyle may lead to the suppression of their natural curiosity, inhibiting their overall cognitive and intellectual development.

Family plays a significant role in a child's development as well. However, family units in the world of child fame can be warped. Parents are seen more as managers, decisions are made on the balance sheet's weight rather than the child's wellbeing, and siblings can become rivals in the race for more fame. These circumstances distort a young star's perception of family and relationships, creating emotional conflict and confusion.

Furthermore, growing up in the public eye isn't natural or easy. Child celebrities face pressure to maintain a crafted public image, placing unnecessary stress on their tender shoulders. This pressure often compels them to hide their true selves, creating an identity conflict that continues into their adulthood.

Also, living in constant scrutiny can lead to a fear of committing mistakes. This fear might hinder their risk-taking ability, a critical aspect of learning during childhood. They may become overly cautious, suppressing their innate creativity and spontaneity.

Living under the limelight also grants child celebrities early access to adult experiences. They deal with money, power, flattery, and manipulation far sooner than their peers, which can disrupt their emotional development and maturity. Child stars may develop a distorted sense of reality and struggle to form authentic relationships due to trust issues.

The experience of fame is also often coupled with an unstable lifestyle. Movie shoots, concerts, promotional events - these can happen anywhere in the world, causing a young star to constantly move around, further adding to the emotional instability.

In a nutshell, the constraints faced by child celebrities are unique and complex. Whereas childhood should be about freedom and exploration, their's is marked by anticipation, expectation, and obligation. Being thrust into structures that cater to their stardom rather than their development, these young stars unfortunately set forth into adulthood without the tools that ease the transition.

Physical Impact of Early Fame

The collateral damage of early fame isn't just psychological; it takes a significant physical toll as well. It's common to see child celebrities struggle with maintaining healthy growth and development due to the unique situations and pressures that come with their high-profile lifestyles.

Handling the physical demands of fame, long working hours, and the continuous scrutiny of the masses challenges a young star's well-being. Metabolism and normal physical development can suffer from continued stress and a lifestyle that doesn't involve regular meals, structured sleep schedules, and sufficient rest periods.

Child celebrities are often required to maintain a particular image, which might mean keeping up with unrealistic beauty standards. The constant pressure to look 'perfect' can lead to unhealthy dietary habits, body image issues, and in severe cases, eating disorders. These youngsters are thrust into an adult world at a tender age where their minds and bodies are still developing, leading to a clash between realistic childhood growth patterns and the demands of spotlight appearance.

Pressure to perform consistently can prompt overuse injuries, which are common among young celebrities, particularly those involved in physically demanding roles or activities. Over time, this repetitive stress on young bodies can lead to chronic conditions that require intensive and potentially dangerous treatments.

Physical absence from school due to irregular working hours can also impact a child's physical development significantly. Physical education classes in schools play a crucial role in a child's growth, emphasizing the importance of movement, exercise, and team sports. In contrast, a 'home-schooled' celebrity child may not have access to these benefits, leading to a less active lifestyle.

Child stars are also exposed to environments relatively more hazardous than an average child's. Late-night shoots, exposure to artificial lighting, or substance abuse can all affect their natural growth patterns and sleep routines.

Substitute a child's playground time with time before the camera, and you've got a recipe for denied physical development opportunities.

Unstructured playtime is essential for a child, not just for their enjoyment but also for the development of gross motor skills, coordination, and physical fitness. In contrast, a child celebrity's work schedule may eliminate this crucial aspect of growing up.

The effects of these pressures materialize not just during their childhood, but also carry well over into their adulthood. Early onset of chronic health problems, stunted growth, or irreversible damage due to substance abuse are some heavy prices paid for early fame.

Young stars often suffer from depleted natural immunity due to the grueling schedules and chronic stress. Frequent bouts of illness, sleep deprivation, suppressed appetite – all are common physical manifestations of the struggle that comes with growing up in the limelight.

The continuous pressure to thrive in an environment that's relentlessly competitive can cause child stars to resort to artificial stimulants and drugs. The stories of young celebrities succumbing to fatal overdoses underline the destructive path that these innocent lives are steered onto.

The stress doesn't end here. Amidst competing with their peers, maintaining an industry-standard physique, and coping with the physical pressures of performing, child celebrities often lose out on personal time necessary for self-growth, reflection, and genuine human interaction.

In conclusion, while the sheen of fame and success might be alluring, the physical costs that come with it are profoundly taxing, especially for young stars. Physiological burnout, chronic health problems, developing dependency on harmful substances - these are just the tip of the iceberg when discussing the physical impact of early fame on child celebrities.

Understanding these consequences is a step towards realizing the importance of proper support structures for young talents. Child labor laws, meticulously designed work schedules, psychological and physical health screenings, and encouraging work-life balance are some of the few changes that can revolutionize the way our society tends to its budding stars.

Childhood is a time for growth and exploration, and while these young talents are indeed unique, it's vital to maintain that they are children first, celebrities second. The physical impact of their premature fame is a stark reminder that their well-being should always come before the glitz and glamour of the spotlight.

The Stress and Strain Manifested As the glaring spotlight of fame casts longer and longer shadows on the lives of child stars, the physical toll they endure under the strain becomes painfully evident. Similar to an overworked machine, their bodies and minds experience the manifestation of stress in various forms. But unlike machines, these child stars can't simply be turned off when things spiral out of control.

Ever seen a starlet with dark circles under her eyes, a washed-out complexion or an uncharacteristic weight change? These are not quirks or eccentricities. They are the product of insomnia, irregular nutrition, intense pressure and potentially a cocktail of performance-enhancement drugs used to cope with the unceasing demands of fame. It can't be stressed enough, beyond the glamorous façade resides a child who is tirelessly working to keep up the pace in a relentless treadmill of celebrity life. The cost of this is grave, it impacts the physical health of young individuals long before their growth period is over. The vicious cycle involves the strain to keep working, an escalating stress level, physical manifestations of stress and eventual burnout, only to begin anew.

To make matters worse, these physical signs of stress are sometimes glamorized as the 'celebrity aura', creating a warped image of a successful star. The sad reality is these are cries for help, a clear sign that young stars are having difficulty coping with their extraordinary circumstances. The irony lies in the fact, for most of us gazing adoringly at them, we see only the glittering fame and fortune, seldom do we recognize the broken shards of their childhood that lie beneath their gilded exterior. The intense physical stress they undergo is largely ignored, and its grave impact on their health, vastly underestimated.

Stars Too Soon: The Psychological Impact

Kids are meant to be kids, right? Their minds should be filled with doodles, dreams and occasionally, homework. Instead, imagine a child buried under the crush of public scrutiny, the weight of fame replacing innocence. Now imagine this weight repeated every single day -- that's the reality for child celebrities.

Fame walks into life, wearing flashy shoes and a dazzling smile, promising the world for a penny. But what it fails to highlight in its fine print is the psychological burden it brings on its young carriers. It doesn't talk about how the soft, growing minds are, more often than not, not prepared to handle this baggage. And how could they be? After all, we're talking about children who've barely learned to tie their shoelaces properly, expected to smoothly navigate the convoluted world of fame.

Child celebrities, by the virtue of their public presence, are bereft of the luxury of a private evolution. Each hiccup, every mistake is amplified for the world to dissect and discuss. Their adolescent angst is no longer a phase; it's a public spectacle. This can result in an amplified stress level, leading to heightened sensitivity or harsh self-criticism. It's akin to growing up inside a pressure cooker, with the world eagerly peeking inside.

Moreover, what's often understated is that the nature of celebrity culture builds a misplaced sense of self-worth. A young mind is taught that their worth is tied to the fluctuating public opinion, to the engagement on their social media posts, to the constant media coverage. This media coverage, both adulation and criticism, can aggressively chip away at a young person's self-esteem.

Remember, these are young talents who're still navigating their own identities, trying to discover where they fit in the world. And while with fame they get a shortcut to being known, they lose out on knowing themselves. They're gnawed by the questions: Do people love me for me or for the celebrity I am? Who am I without my fame? Is my true self enough?

Further, it's essential to realize that young celebrities, bar their fame, are just like any other child. They crave validation, acceptance, belongingness... And rightly so, as these are fundamental human needs. But fame and acceptance don't necessarily go hand in hand. While they might be accepted by their fans for their craft, they can often feel isolated in their personal lives. This sense of not belonging, coupled with the duty to maintain a public persona, can create an internal disconnect leaving them emotionally vulnerable.

A cocktail of such psychological complexities is consuming for an adult, let alone a child still understanding emotions. This often results in outbursts, rebellions, and the need to self-express in ways that aren't always accepted by society. However, they are less about the 'troubled child' stereotype and more about the noise and confusion of growing up too fast, too soon.

Being a child star isn't just about performing under the spotlight; it's about living under it too. In such a scenario, the stage blurs with reality, and artifice can replace authenticity. This imposition of a prematurely formed identity can be a harsh intrusion into their psychological development, leaving a long-lasting impact.

Truth be told, these are children thrust into an adult universe, burdened with adult-sized expectations. Evolving amidst this whirlwind of fame's harsh spotlight, it's their raw, inherent resilience that becomes their lifeline, helping them balance on the tightrope of stardom.

The Increments of Psychological Burden are a harsh reality for young individuals under the glaring sky of fame. Can we understand the color and weight of this burden? Imagine for a moment the dazzling lights of stardom consistently beckoning the tender minds of child celebrities; it's not as delightful as one may fantasize. There's a definite charm that fame casts, no doubt, but it doesn't come without massive psychological ramifications. And these aren't all at once, but rather pile onto young stars in incremental doses, making it even more strenuous to deal with.

"How?" you might wonder. Well, it begins with an erosion of privacy, a constant swarm of paparazzi and fans, a ceaseless scrutiny by the media, and an almost omnipresent public pressure of maintaining an idealistic image. All of these gradually push the child stars into a vortex of anxiety, depression, and feeling isolated from reality. What's even worse, this may result in them behaving erratically or rebelling, not out of teenage unpredictability, but as a desperate cry for help or a need to mark their identity outside their stardom.

It's a paradox. Stardom bestows on them an almost godlike status, leaving no further place to escalate to, leading to a stagnation in personal achievements that is difficult for them to cope with. Therefore, in many cases, child celebrities are often pushed into adulthood prematurely as they must manage hefty professional responsibilities that their peers are unfamiliar with; causing them to miss out on important developmental stages, resulting in a deep-seated sense of loss. Thus, it's fair to say that the psychological toll fame takes on child stars is massive and that the further we look, the more loops of this complex maze are unravelled. This is not to say that fame is entirely damaging. However, it is imperative that we acknowledge and address the substantial psychological burden it can pose for our young stars.

Chapter 3:
Child Stars and Mental Health

The roller coaster of child stardom is one that's often marked by sharp highs and aggressive dips, blitzing young minds with an overwhelming surge of emotions and experiences. There's a fair bit of glamour, sure. But the bright lights cast long shadows that tend to cloak the more poignant aspect of a child star's life — mental health. It's necessary to take a psychiatric glance into young Hollywood and understand how stardom profoundly affects their kaleidoscope of mental stability. And this isn't just about one or two rogue elements. The spotlight, for all its warmth, often burns and maims the fragile psyche of the youngest showbiz members, sometimes making casualties out of the most promising ones. The implicit danger, a suppressed trauma, is very real. These little stars carry a Pandora's Box filled to the brim with immense hidden trauma, waiting to spill and shatter their innocence. As such, in our attempt to demystify the luminous world of child stars, we cannot afford to overlook or underestimate the profound impacts this life has on these budding minds—as well as the psychological scars invariably etched onto the fabric of their upbringing.

The Couch Talks - Psychoanalysis of Child Stars is a fascinating delve into the minds of young celebs, dissecting, and understanding the emotional and psychological aspects that unravel behind the façade of the glitz and glamour. The burdens of fame and the limelight cast upon these young stars serve as a unique stressor on their psyche, far detached from the everyday stresses faced by their less famous peers.

The glittering world of show business promises a smorgasbord of privileges and spoils, yet it simultaneously strips child stars of an essential aspect of their life - the freedom to grow, explore, and create on their own terms. What it presents instead is a tightly bound universe, clouded by constant public scrutiny and unrealistic expectations.

The compulsion to fit into a specific mold and demonstrate an air of maturity beyond their years wreaks havoc on their mental wellbeing, leading to anxiety, depression, and an array of other mental health disorders. These enfant terribles of the movie world are pushed to perform at their optimal best round the clock, a bar too high even for an adult, let alone a budding child. As a result, they are torn between juggling their booming career and the stark realities of their everyday life, which is far from normal.

This relentless pressure, coupled with the lack of space for confiding or expressing their fears, leads to a buildup of suppressed emotions. In most cases, the ultimate outlet for these emotions manifests as public outbursts, a desperate cry for help that often goes unheard or is trivialized as a 'tantrum'. Decoding these 'tantrums' and recognizing them as an indication of their internal conflicts, confusion, and stress is the first step in unmasking their true agony.

Acknowledging the gravity of these issues, it demands an immediate behavioural and societal change. By providing these child celebs with necessary channels for discussing their stressors openly, a shift in perception about young stars can take place. It's not their extravagant wealth or possessions that need the spotlight, but their mental wellbeing which should be the primary focus. Easing the burden of fame on these growing minds can ultimately lead to healthier, brighter child stars who gradually evolve into well-rounded, mature individuals with voices of their own, devoid of the psychological scars that the world of glamour often inflicts.

How Fame Influences Mental Stability

Rolling along with our analysis, the next major component under review is the way fame inadvertently weaves itself into the mental stability of child stars. To grasp a concept as complex as fame's direct impact on the mental health of young celebrities, we have to look at fame not as a superficial phenomenon, but as a life-altering experience.

On the surface, fame adorns the star with glitz and popularity, but beneath that shimmering facade, fame's impact can be daunting. The exorbitant pressure and constant public scrutiny child stars face can toy with their mental stability, often causing cognitive and emotional distress. This often interferes with the normal developmental milestones, contributing to a sort of skewed reality.

A vital point to remember is the direct correlation between fame and power. A sudden surge in popularity often thrusts child stars into a realm of immense power and control. While this might sound thrilling, the paradox turns apparent when you realize that power isn't suited to a developing mind that's yet to learn self-restraint and responsibility.

As a result, this abrupt leap can lead to a cognitive disarray that aggravates feelings of anxiety and insecurity, disrupting their sense of self. This often manifests in a disrupted self-esteem, signs of depression, and other psychological issues, creating a significant crisis in their mental stability.

Without a proper outlet or tool to handle such overwhelming pressures, they are often left feeling isolated. Isolation, coupled with constant scrutiny from every angle, exacerbates their anxieties, pushing them deeper into the abyss of mental instability.

Fame, by its very nature, is also ephemeral and uncertain. One day you're the talk of the town, and the next, you may be irrelevant. Alice, a 10-year-old TV sensation, might have to grapple with the reality that her fame may not last into her teens. This uncertainty can cultivate a constant fear within young stars. Therefore, the fear of obscurity, combined with the pressure to maintain relevance, can have profound consequences on their mental health.

Then there's the issue of privacy, or rather the lack thereof. Picture yourself under the spotlight every living moment, with your every move being analyzed by the world. Seems overwhelming, right? Child stars often struggle to form a clear boundary between their public persona and actual self, which can lead to identity crises, further threatening their mental stability.

Let's not forget the ugly reality where fame becomes a breeding ground for substance abuse in a bid to escape the constant pressures and criticisms. It can be a vicious cycle – fame leads to mental turmoil, and substance abuse provides a short-lived solace, which eventually fuels the mental instability.

Lastly, but significantly, the absence of a safe, non-judgemental space where they can express their fears, voids, and concerns can compound these issues. Even the brightest limelight can cast the darkest shadows, and it's in these unilluminated corners where the mental health of our child stars are often ignored and compromised.

In a nutshell, fame is not the culprit, but a catalyst that can influence mental stability. Expanding our view from an exaggerated Hollywood scandal to a more benign understanding of the psychological implications of fame, it's evident that being thrust into the limelight can impose burdens far beyond the sparkly appearance.

The Implicit Danger: Suppressed Trauma

When we open the pages of a celebrity magazine or turn our TV screens to the glamorous Hollywood, we witness a world filled with glamour and opulence. Yet, this exuberant exterior often masks a grim reality - the suppressed trauma of child stars. In an industry that demands constant performance and perfection, it isn't abnormal for these youthful talents to overlook their internal struggles, burying their traumas beneath layers of pretense and make-believe.

From a young age, child stars grapple with an unordinary life. They're thrust into an adult world of immense pressure and high stakes. Picking up cues from their experienced senior stars and managers, they master the skill of concealing their true emotions and fears, quickly becoming adept actors in their lives, not just on the screen. This suppression of emotions and traumatic instances can, unfortunately, result in severe implications for their mental health in the long run.

Consider the expectations placed on a child star. There is a high demand to deliver optimum performances, often at the expense of regular childhood experiences. Let's take the pressures to maintain a particular image, expected cuts in personal and social life, and the often excessive scrutiny by media and public into perspective. Now, imagine facing all of it while still trying to navigate the typical challenges of growing up. It's a double-edged sword – while they're persistently under the public gaze, their internal battles stay alarmingly invisible, bubbling beneath the surface.

Vulnerability and mental exhaustion might arise as these young individuals strive to meet the expectations of a demanding public. In efforts to keep up appearances and maintain their crafted image, they might suppress negative feelings or emotional distress, inadvertently creating an internal time bomb of pent-up trauma. This suppression and neglect of their emotional health often amplify their feelings of loneliness, anxiety, and depression.

The powerful correlation between trauma and mental health in child stars is further evidenced by their emergence into adulthood. By then, their suppressed trauma and unresolved emotional distress may lead them down a path of dysfunctional coping mechanisms, such as substance abuse or self-destructive behavior. These mechanisms, though damaging, are desperate attempts to cope with the overwhelming feelings of trauma that they've carried throughout their early years in the spotlight.

What exacerbates this issue is the disregard of their inner turmoil by those around them. The entourage that surrounds these child stars, including managers, agents, and sometimes even family, are often more focused on their exterior achievements and escalating careers than on their interior battles. This ignorance can add to their sense of isolation and loneliness, further fuelling their suppressed trauma.

In such situations, even when a child star has the courage to voice their internal struggles, it's often dismissed or downplayed under the guise of 'part and parcel' of their chosen career, thus normalizing their pain. This attitude is not just callously dismissive, but it also discourages these young superstars from seeking help, consequently pushing them further into the quagmire of their suppressed trauma and emotional turmoil.

Moreover, the societal lens views successful child stars as fortunate beings. To the public eye, their fairytale journey seems to be devoid of hardships, further discouraging these stars from showcasing any signs of emotional distress. The fear of rejection, mockery, and loss of public goodwill forces them to continue treading the path of pretense - a mask that hides their suffering smiles.

In concluding, while the captivating allure of child stardom casts a bewitching spell on many, it becomes crucial to shed light on the impending risks that shadow this path. The suppression of trauma is an inadvertent by-product of their unique lifestyle, constructing an invisible barrier between their glamorous public image and the turmoil within. It is incumbent upon us, as empathetic viewers and ardent fans, to not just celebrate their successes but also address and lend an understanding ear to their struggles to ensure their mental health is not cast aside as an inconspicuous casualty of their stardom.

Unboxing the Pandora's Box: Hidden Trauma Peel back the glitz of the red carpet, and we unveil a darker reality lurking in the shadows of fame. Young celebrities, thrown into the deep end of the fame pool, often carry hidden traumas that underpin their actions and reactions. More than just a Pandora's box filled with seemingly outlandish behavior, these are psychological wounds embedded deeply into their budding minds.

Uncovered, these traumas make their existence clear in bouts of rebellion, erratic behavior, addiction spirals, and other symptoms. They are symbols of torment nurtured by the relentless pressure of the spotlight. Fame can come with presumptions, invasions, a stolen childhood, and an arena-sized expectation that could overwhelm even the most adept adults. For adolescent celebrities, they are dealing with these heavyweight challenges even before they can build emotional resilience, creating a bubble of unchecked trauma that's waiting to rupture.

One can't just tape over these jarring cracks with more fame and expect them not to bulge under pressure. Instead, the industry, with all its power and influence, needs to take a step back and rethink the collateral damage of fame. From stage parents to studio executives, from societal voyeurism to media mosquito swarms; the Pandora's box, once unleashed, can't easily be closed. Better then, to not let it fester into a powder keg of misdemeanors, depression, or worse. This highlights the impelling requirement for psychological support, a robust industry reform, and a fundamental shift in how we perceive and treat our child stars.

Chapter 4:
Public Outbursts: A Child Star's Silent Cry

When a well-known celebrity lashes out, it often becomes breaking news and headline fodder. The initial shock and fascination quickly morph into an insatiable appetite for all the gory details. However, when we peel back the layers of sensationalism, mayhem and exhaustive commentary, we find a poignant tale of vulnerability and distress at the heart of these outbursts. Especially concerning child stars, these public spectacles can often be the visible side of a deeply hidden struggle. It's an external manifestation of the quandaries they face growing up in an unforgiving limelight that doesn't allow for the mistakes most kids are allowed to make and learn from. The fame-infused environment they grow up in can make them more susceptible to outbursts compared to kids who experience a typical upbringing. The spotlight, suffused with public expectations and relentless scrutiny, amplifies each misstep they take. For child stars, throwing tantrums, resorting to substance abuse, or engaging in reckless behavior can be a kind of silent cry, an urgent appeal for understanding, help or a desperate craving to reclaim their stolen childhoods. Instead of just gawking or passing judgment, it's vital to decode their silent plea and realize what's actually at stake. These outbursts are often symptoms of deeper underlying issues, overwhelmed by expectations, the lack of personal agency, and the pressure to forever please and perform. By understanding this, we can see these public outbursts for what they often truly are: a child star's silent cry for space, understanding, and support.

Comparing Public Outbursts: Celebrities vs Non-celebrities

Continuing from our exploration of public outbursts as a child star's silent cry, let's probe deeper into a comparative analysis between celebrity outbursts and those from non-famed individuals. The sharp contrast and notable similarities will shed light on how fame significantly influences these meltdowns.

The social media age has amplified our awareness of celebrity missteps to an unprecedented level. Every misstep, every controversial tweet, and every public altercation becomes a trending news story faster than ever before. Now, keeping in mind this heightened scrutiny, let's parallel it with the outbursts of the average American adolescent.

Teen years are often tumultuous. They stand as a critical period of identity formation, self-assertion, and exploring boundaries. It's worth noting that outbursts, acting out, and rebellious behavior are common among non-celebrity teenagers. In essence, these bursts are typical forms of self-expression that allow teenagers to voice their frustrations or to simply push societal norms.

Just like non-celebrity teenagers, child celebrities also experience these universal adolescent pressures. However, they endure an added layer of complexity due to their public status. When fame is thrown into the mix, the pressure cooker environment it creates tends to multiply the intensity of their outbursts.

Contrasts emerge starkly when an average teenager's public outbursts are compared with those of celebrities. For a non-celebrity teenager, outbursts might result in high school gossip or a stern talking-to from parents or teachers. But for child celebrities, such actions can create entertainment news headlines, stir wide-scale public condemnations, and even impact career opportunities.

What turns the dial up even further is the expectation for child celebrities to maintain a faultless, picture-to-perfect public image that distinctly contrasts the normal, messy process of adolescence. There's an implicit understanding that they must always be "on," ready for public scrutiny, the minute they step out of their home. The pressure to conform to this perfect image is immense.

A striking similarity between the public outbursts of celebrities and non-celebrital adolescents is the fundamental reason hiding behind these meltdowns. Whether you're in the glaring public eye or living an anonymous life, adolescence often brings forth confusion, anxiety, or frustration, leading to such outbursts.

But let's remember that contrary to non-celebrities, famous adolescents have less room to hide or recover from their mistakes. Their outbursts become frozen permanently in public memory, or worse, on the internet. This lack of a safety net can exacerbate their pressure and potentially lead to escalated outbursts, something the average teenager would not experience.

Another key difference to focus upon is the exchange of privacy for fame. Unlike their non-celebrity counterparts, child stars do not have the luxury of 'slipping up' in private. Long after their outburst is over and their anger subsided, the evidence potentially remains, circulating the virtual world, sparking conversations, unlike the experiences of an average teenager.

Understanding the shared yet varied experiences of youthful outbursts goes a long way in showing compassion towards child celebrities while they navigate through this challenging phase. We must learn to appreciate that child stars, like all young people, are prone to making mistakes. But, subjected to the intense pressure of the limelight, they bear a heavier burden.

At the heart of it, child celebrities are just kids learning to navigate the world. But unlike the average teenager, they're doing so under the ruthless microscope of fame. The public needs to realize that child stars aren't prop characters but real people experiencing their adolescence, just in a far less forgiving environment.

Comparing public outbursts of non-celebrities and celebrities undeniably reveals that the world of fame has unique problems and pressures. However, it also shows how strikingly similar they can be to their non-famed counterparts in many ways. Ultimately, this suggests that we must apply a softer lens, acknowledging not just the differences, but also the universality, when scrutinizing their public outbursts.

The societal obsession with the lives of the famous exacerbates these issues, making a celebrity's journey through adolescence disproportionately challenging. So, let us explore further in the next chapter about the dynamics of the publicity market surrounding public meltdowns, understand its intricacies, and undertake a more compassionate lens towards the behavior and actions of our—young and under pressure—stars.

The Market of Public Meltdowns makes an uncomfortable read - we're talking about child celebrities, after all. But let's take a deeper dive into it. Over time, a somewhat twisted market has formed around the public meltdowns of young celebs. This marketplace thrives on spectacle and drama, and every display of hysteria or ill-judged behavior is promptly cashed in by the ever-present paparazzi and tabloid media.

As society becomes more voyeuristic and internet culture more relentless, these episodes of outlash are amplified and spread like wildfire across the globe. Invariably, when such a meltdown occurs, there's a period of a few days or a week when the child celeb becomes the center of everyone's universe. We've seen this pattern play out time and again. The moment a child star steps out of line, the media circus descends, ready to pounce on every scandalous or shocking detail, distorting and amplifying it until it's front-page news.

What's more unnerving is that this 'marketplace' doesn't just exploit these public breakdowns, but also anticipates and encourages them. Society has an unusually macabre fascination with the fall from grace - the higher the rise, the harder the fall. And for child celebrities in the merciless glare of the spotlight, this can result in an alarming amount of pressure. Yes, it's an uncomfortable truth about society's perverse appetite for spectacle. This market of public meltdowns, although both morbid and concerning, is one of the ramifications of childhood fame, another facet we need to scrutinize and address appropriately in nurturing young talents.

The Cry Behind the Outrage Understandably, when we witness young celebrities having public meltdowns, we may write it off as youthful rebellion or a sign of weakness. However, dig a little deeper and we find something quite different, we find a silent cry echoing deep within the caverns of their tormented psyche. It's not as much a gutsy act of defiance as it is a desperate plea for help, understanding, and a longing for a normal life.

What we often refer to as outrageous is frequently an elusive attempt to raise a voice against their just-as-outrageous circumstances. Remember, these young stars are still kids, handling pressures and demands most adults would find daunting. The perpetual publicity, the constant scrutiny of their actions, words, relationships, or appearance creates a strain that very few could fully comprehend. Furthermore, the pressure to fulfill the expectations of fans, directors, and even their family often leads to an emotional breakdown. This takes the tragic form of public emotional outbursts and sometimes even physical altercations.

So, when next we see a young celebrity lose their cool in public, let's not hastily judge or label them as spoiled brats. Instead, let's pause and remember that we're seeing the draining effect of continuous pressure and expectations. We're witnessing the mental cracks beneath the limelight, the unseen scars from numerous disappointments and betrayals, the tears from the public's unreasonable expectations, and the losses of normality. It is pivotal to understand that their outbursts are not signs of weakness or entitlement but rather symptoms of the psychological burdens they're shouldering. It's not a call for mockery, it's their cry for help.

Chapter 5:
Parental Influence and the Child Celebrity

The role parents play in the lives of child celebrities is undoubtedly substantial and pivotal. The childhoods of these young stars are shaped in the hands of individual influencers who either act as protective shields or are swayed by the lure of profit. It's a precarious tightrope to walk, this balance between caregiving and exploitation. In an industry that rides high on vulnerability and exposure, a misstep on part of the parents can catapult child stars into uncharted territories of public outbursts and personal turmoil. When parents fail in their role as safe harbors, the disturbing waves of Hollywood's turbulent sea toss and turn the young navigators within, often leading to public tantrums that echo their silent cries for help.

Contemplating effective parenting styles raises the perennial debate between helicopter and free-range approaches. It's a dichotomy between relentless supervision and fostering independence, but the turbulent nature of showbiz requires a bespoke, hybrid style. Navigating the choppy waters of child stardom calls for a balance - a protective vigil that doesn't smother, and a freedom that doesn't abandon. Parenting a child celebrity is an art that demands constant calibrations, an understanding ear, and an empathetic heart - because beneath their stardust-sprinkled personas, celebrities are still children who need guidance and love. A healthy parental influence, therefore, plays an imperative role in steering these young stars away from the reefs of public outbursts and toward the harbor of positive mental health.

Hollywood Parents: Protectors or Profiteers?

Fame is a double-edged sword, and the sharp end often points towards those who get a taste of the limelight too early in their lives - the child celebrities. Overseeing these young talents are their parents, all too often thrust into a spotlight they're not usually equipped to handle. Are these parents protectors or profiteers? It's a contentious subject worth exploring.

On one hand, many parents genuinely wish to support their children's interests and passions. This gesture of unconditional love can morph into the role of their child's manager, a position of immense responsibility that is often fraught with challenges. Charged with handling their child's work load, press appearances, contracts, wages, they're constantly walking on a tight line balancing between their parental duties and showbiz obligations.

On the other side of the spectrum, you have parents who see the earning potential in their child's budding talent and seek to capitalize on it. They may argue this is in their child's best interest, securing their financial future and establishing their career early on. But overbearing ambition and monetary goals can lead to exploitation. From taking excessively large portions of their earnings to pushing them beyond their limits, these parents blur the line between providing for and profiteering from their child.

Child actors like Macaulay Culkin have publicly spoken about their complicated relationship with their parents, culminating in legal battles for emancipation and control over their fortunes. Yet, the public rarely gets a clear picture of the true dynamics. The line between support and exploitation often remains blurred, and the courts are left to make difficult decisions about these children's futures.

Many of these child stars are forced into an adult world before they're ready, trading school yards and suburban serenity for work obligations and public scrutiny. The burden of fame is undoubtedly heavy, and when placed on young shoulders, it can lead to all manner of complications, from developmental issues to mental health crises.

For child celebrities, the prying eyes of the public and press can amplify even the simplest family squabbles into scandals. And when parents are also the managers, the line between private familial matters and professional disputes becomes blurred. This adds another dimension of psychological stress that these young stars often struggle to navigate.

The glaring lens of fame also has the power to exacerbate and expose any existing familial issues. Addictions, divorces, abuse or neglect by parents often become tabloid fodder, leading to more scrutiny and stress on the child. Chaotic off-stage drama, combined with the on-camera pressure, can be a poison cocktail for the young star's mental health.

In an industry as unrelenting as Hollywood, the role of parents in a child star's life is far from simple. They are faced with the challenging task of maintaining the delicate balance between their child's fame and their emotional, mental, and physical well-being.

But there are encouraging examples too, where parents have successfully managed to guide their children through the turbulence of TV and movie stardom, transitioning into mature, well-rounded individuals who have learned to cope with their fame instead of being consumed by it. So, not all Hollywood parents fall neatly into the exploitative category.

The parents' ability to keep their child's best interest at heart - prioritizing their well-being over their career - plays a crucial role in deciding whether they'll be protectors or profiteers. At the end of the day, navigating the maze of fame, success, and the pitfalls that come with it, requires much more than starry-eyed ambition.

For these reasons, the question of whether parents of child stars are protectors or profiteers is complex. Although there are certainly cases of both spectrums, greater scrutiny and reform are necessary to protect the industry's most vulnerable.

In the world of Hollywood, the need for ethical guardianship and management is paramount. Parents, as well as the broader industry community, have a responsibility to navigate the ambition and potential, always remembering that these stars are children first.

Constant education and informative resources regarding industry transparency, fair contracts and mental health support for children in show business should be made accessible to the parents. This can provide them the guidance required to keep their nurturing parental instincts intact while their child traverses in this flashy yet potent Hollywood landscape.

In conclusion, the world of childhood stardom is far from simple, and the role of the parents is a pivotal one. While it's easy to categorize Hollywood parents as either protectors or profiteers, the truth is inevitably far more nuanced. It's crucial to have open dialogues around these complexities, so we can better understand and support these young stars and the challenges they face.

The Thin Line between Care and Exploitation finds its roots in a deeply entangled web of love, ambition, and dollar signs that often misshape the parental role in a young star's life. A parent of a child star needs to navigate a muddled terrain that is governed by a heart-felt parental desire to feather a nurturing nest and an equally compelling urge to cash on the golden goose that stardom potentially promises.

We see a stark contrast in the economic dynamics of a typical American household and that of a celebrity child. Ordinary parents, in their nurturing roles, may strive to save for their children's college tuition or to secure their future, whereas the parents of child stars are faced with the unique economic reality where the income roles are reversed. Their kids may be the primary breadwinners of the family. This reverse cash flow can breed a perplexing mix of pride, guilt, and dependency, creating extremely complex dynamics that have the potential to cross over from care to exploitation without even realizing it.

The fuzzy line of control between hedged-in guidance and outright exploitation often stems from the incessant public scrutiny and harsh spotlight that is relentlessly shone on the tiny shoulders of these budding stars. Parents find themselves wrestling with a dual role of a manager and a guardian, a balance which proves difficult to maintain. Consequently, we witness unfortunate cases where the guardian aspect takes a backseat, and the manager persona takes over, leading to adverse childhood experiences, leaving child stars grappling with feelings of being used and betrayed by those they most trusted. The challenge here is to ensure the protection of childhood innocence while also honoring the demands of the star life – a daunting tightrope to tread indeed.

The Role of Parents in Celebrity Outbursts

As we delve further into the influences shaping child celebrities' experiences, parents come into sharp focus. The parents of these young stars are perhaps the most influential figures in their lives. They're not just parents; they're managers, coaches, public relations reps all rolled up into one, and their actions can certainly contribute to the public outbursts their famous offspring are often seen making.

For starters, many celebrity parents often transition into a role more akin to a manager than a conventional caregiver. In their well-intentioned attempt at guiding their child's career, they may inadvertently prioritize professional commitments over personal growth and development. This shifting of organization often results in an imbalance in the child's life which can contribute to emotional stressors leading up to potential outbursts.

Many times, children celebrities are not encouraged to express negative emotions at home, as their personas are associated with their professional brand. Encouraged to maintain an image of constant positivity and success, these young stars often repress frustrations or anger. When this emotional pressure build-up finds an outlet, it often results in a volcanic public eruption, casting a stark contrast to their meticulously curated public image.

Additionally, some parents of child celebrities may inadvertently exploit the talents of their children for personal gain, blurring the boundaries between the child's individual identity and their professional persona. When a child's individual identity is overshadowed, they may use public outbursts as a way to reclaim that lost aspect of self, an attempt to differentiate between who they truly are and the character they play in the public eye.

Sometimes, parents unwittingly contribute to their child's public meltdowns by failing to establish and maintain normalcy in their day-to-day lives. A typical childhood and adolescence provide opportunities for young individuals to learn important life skills, make mistakes, and understand their boundaries. These experiences are, more often than not, missed by child celebrities. Their skewed perspective of normality feeds into their inability to handle disappointments and failures, further ratcheting up their potential for public outbursts.

When a child celebrity starts experiencing fame at a young age, their understanding of the world and the expectations of them may become warped. Their parents, who should ideally buffer them against the harsh realities of the entertainment industry, may end up reinforcing it. This environment intensifies their feelings of helplessness and frustration, potentially triggering volatile outbursts as a misguided means of asserting control over their own lives.

It's also worth noting that in many cases, the over-involvement or under-involvement of parents can exacerbate a child celebrity's emotional instability. The constant scrutiny of helicopter parenting can lead the child to act out in rebellion, seeking attention or an escape from the constrictions of their controlled environment. On the other hand, a free-range approach can give the impression of neglect, having the child feel lost or unsupported, which can also cause emotional turmoil, often projected into the public sphere.

However, it isn't all doom and gloom. There are instances where parents maintain a healthy balance amid an uncommon situation. By preserving a sense of normalcy at home, encouraging open communication, ensuring their child has time for relaxation and friends, and providing an education outside of the entertainment business, they manage to avoid the pitfalls of celebrity upbringing. These parents realize their role isn't just to manage their child's career, but to also guide them in successfully navigating their peculiar circumstances.

However, such cases are sadly the exception rather than the rule. The role of parents in child celebrity outbursts is multidimensional and complex. It's a circumstance where the lines between personal and public, child and professional, normal and extraordinary are constantly blurred. It's a tightrope walk, where any misstep can lead to mishaps, which are often magnified in the form of public outbursts.

At the end of the day, parents of child celebrities bear a significant, albeit not sole, responsibility for their offsprings' actions. The connection between a celebrity child's public outbursts and their parental influences serves as a crucial reminder to all parents - celebrity or not - about the importance of maintaining a nurturing and balanced environment for the growth and well-being of their children.

When Parents Drop the Ball ...

Truth be told, sometimes parents can blunder by not providing an adequate support system for their child stars, unintentionally contributing to the child's emotional and psychological turmoil. Emotional neglect is all too common in the glitz and glamour world of Hollywood. Parents, blinded by the star-power of their children, might end up prioritizing their child's professional obligations over their emotional needs. This lack of emotional support can cause young celebrities to feel isolated and misunderstood, eventually leading them to act out as a cry for help.

Now, don't get me wrong, no parents intentionally harm their kids. However, the allure of fame and fortune can distort good judgement. Parents, despite their best intentions, may misplace their protective instincts, focusing on the financial and fame-driven benefits of their child's career over their child's overall well-being. Consequently, these child celebrities may grow up feeling their worth is tied to their public persona and professional success, rather than to who they are as individuals. This psychological misalignment can significantly contribute to the public outbursts we often see play out in the media.

Moreover, it's important to acknowledge the precarious position these parents themselves are thrust into. No parenting book can equip you with how to handle the beast that is stardom. The pressures, responsibilities, and sacrifices associated with having a child in the spotlight can be immense and overwhelming. Without proper guidance and support, it's all too easy for parents to make missteps. But when these parental missteps are made in the world of young celebrities, they're made in a very public eye, amplifying the consequences for all involved. For all the nifty gadgets and glimmering trophies that fame brings, it can often extract a hefty price from those unprepared to navigate its complexities.

Helicopter vs. Free-Range: The Best Parenting Style for Child Stars

Navigating the choppy seas of fame is tricky, especially for celebrities who are thrown into its whirlwinds from a young age. It ain't a walk in the park, and for many child stars, their coping mechanism and reaction to fame is often influenced significantly by their parents' style. Are helicopter parents, always hovering and ever vigilant, best suited for this delicate parenting role? Or perhaps the free-range style, defined by less strict supervision and more emphasis on a child's independence, prevails as the preferable parenting methodology in Hollywood?

When we're talking about child stars in particular, we are dealing with uniquely complex lifestyle situations. The heightened level of attention and pressure that comes with early notoriety puts them in an outlying spot of vulnerability. Perhaps because of this, strictly traditional parenting strategies might not be the most appropriate choice. This is where a more customized, mixed-style approach to parenting may be needed.

Let's consider helicopter parents first. In the highly volatile and unpredictable world of showbiz, having a protective force ready to swoop in might not be such a bad thing. They can provide a much-needed line of defense against exploitative agents or unwelcome negative media attention. Helicopter parenting, characterized by strict surveillance and intense involvement, often applies constant pressure on the child. Yet, this pressure might be helpful for some child stars, establishing structure in a field that is often lacking it.

On the flip side, though, the heavy-handed presence of helicopter parents could stifle the growth of a child star's personal identity and independence, essential traits in navigating showbiz, let alone life in general. Following their parents' directed path might lead child stars to become detached from their true passions, emotional development, and self-discovery. The ever-present eye of the helicopter parent, while providing protective cover, may also cast a long shadow over personal growth.

Shift the lens onto free-range parenting, and we see a counterpoint to the overly protective. This approach is marked by a notion of 'let the kids be kids'. Free-range parents provide their children with guidance, but prioritize the child's ability to make and learn from their own decisions and mistakes. They are inclined to give their celebrity children a choice, allowing them to experience a taste, albeit skewed, of normality within their extraordinary lives.

Despite the benefits of fostering independence and self-reliance, this hands-off approach could have its pitfalls when it comes to child stars. With less supervision, kids might be more susceptible to the potential predatory aspects of the industry. This style may pose additional risks of rebellious outbursts or risky behavior - a result of a perceived lack of structure and boundaries.

So, which parenting style wins out in the end? Well, asserting that one style is universally superior for all child stars would be a gross oversimplification. Each child star is unique, boasting different personalities, predispositions, and coping mechanisms. As such, the best approach is likely a customized one that integrates favorable aspects from both helicopter and free-range parenting styles - offering support and protection while fostering independent decision-making and growth. It's a balance, a dance if you will, but one of critical importance for ensuring the child's wellbeing in the spotlight.

In the end, parenting a child celebrity requires enduring understanding and patience, alongside an unwavering determination to safeguard the child's welfare and mental health. Careful navigation between the extremes of smothering and neglecting is key. And no matter the style, the foundation of love, compassion and respect is integral to effectively support your child through the roller coaster ride of their early fame.

Remember, a successful child star is not exclusively measured by their career but also by their ability to foster a well-rounded and sound state of mind. This, above all else, is a testament to the role of parents in shaping the futures of their famous offspring. They are, at the end of the day, not just stars but kids trying to find their way in the world.

Navigating the Choppy Seas of Fame is no small feat. Unlike their peers, child stars ride the turbulent waves of showbiz while trying to maintain a semblance of normalcy. Their journey into adulthood is not just about adjusting to hormonal changes or grappling with more challenging schoolwork; it involves publicly fighting stereotypes and pressures that come tied with a bow to their fame.

The inherent instability that comes with navigating the territory of fame can be analogous to a ship in a stormy sea. It's easy to lose direction, to be overwhelmed by the tumultuous environment. They are constantly in the spotlight, with their every move scrutinized. They can't indulge in the usual frivolities like other kids because of tight shooting schedules, or their risky behavior might be plastered in the tabloids the next day. If they misstep or falter, they risk becoming a punchline or a cautionary tale, damaging their career prospects and, more ominously, their self-esteem.

Parents play a crucial role here. They are the lighthouse guiding their famous children through the storm. They need to keep a firm, yet understanding hand on the tiller to steer their children, helping them balance the demands of their career and their need for a normal childhood. But suppose they mistake exploitation for encouragement, or succumb to the allure of fame and money. In that case, their children might drift and lose sight of their true selves, leading to emotional turbulence and public outbursts. The lessons young celebrities learn while navigating these choppy seas ultimately shape who they become, making the journey as important as the destination.

Chapter 6:
Fame, Power, and Abuse in Hollywood

As we delve into the murky waters of fame's underbelly, it becomes glaringly evident that the glimmer of the Hollywood front acts as a smokescreen for much darker realities. The power dynamics in the film industry often fosters an environment that can lead to the exploitation of child stars. Unfortunately, tales of these young celebs facing abuse, both physical and emotional, are tragically all too common. This abuse can be systemic, considering the manipulative tactics that are often employed by industry heavies to intimidate or control these vulnerable stars. Such ordeals paint an alarming picture of how easily fame can be weaponized against the very people it ideally should benefit. However, it's not all pitch dark. There has been a surge in activism and awareness with movements such as #MeToo and Time's Up breaking the silence. What will follow would be an assessment of systemic changes that aim at safeguarding child celebrities from such traumatic experiences. The tides are undoubtedly turning, but there's still a long way to go.

The Unpleasant Side of Stardom: Abuse Stories

Once the camera lights dim and the admiring applause dies down, what is left is the unsavory reality that many child stars have to face. Fame often leads to a life of abuse, both evident and quietly hidden. These children, crammed under the spotlight's stifling heat, are forced to grow up in a world riddled with exploitation, manipulation, neglect, and worse.

It's a discomforting truth that the gleaming facade of Hollywood has a shadowy underside, where the innocence of a budding star is frequently bargained for power and personal gain. Child actors are often targeted for abuse by industry insiders, which commonly leads to psychological struggles.

Remember, these are children, just starting to understand the world around them when they're shoved into a mire of distressing experiences. They must confront sexual harassment, substance abuse, and party atmospheres, issues typically beyond the comprehension and handling capabilities of their young minds. It's an ugly side of stardom that places a massive cloud over their developmental years and may cause severe trauma that continues into adulthood.

Undoubtedly, the subtle and pervasive nature of abuse can make its detection challenging. Many child celebs find it difficult to raise alarm bells due to manipulative tactics employed by the abusers. These cunning figures exploit the power differentials, the young actor's aspirations or fear of career obliteration to shroud their acts under a thick veil of secrecy.

Further complicating the matter is the profound mistrust child stars develop towards authority figures. When the people who are supposed to protect them fail to do so, it feels as though they've been failed by the system. They are isolating themselves, feeling disconnected from reality, and ensnared in a paralyzing cycle of fear and helplessness.

An unfortunate example of this came to light with the rampant child abuse crisis that plagued the film industry. Many ended up living a life wrecked with mental health issues, substance abuse, and an overall inability to lead a normal life beyond the reach of stardom. This reality only underscores the gravity and necessity to address this issue.

Sexual abuse is a particularly insidious form of exploitation. Child stars are often left devastated, their innocence tarnished, trust shattered, and self-esteem decimated. Left unaddressed, these experiences sour their perception of the world, promoting a cynical, defensive, and distrustful approach towards life as they grow older.

Within this grim landscape of abuse lies another beast: emotional manipulation. It can be just as damaging, if not more so, as it undermines the child's mental health and sets the stage for later mental issues. Coercive tactics are applied to control these young individuals, successfully creating a toxicity that permeates their life even after the lights are turned down.

Physical abuse during the early stages of stardom is also a significant concern. This includes excessive discipline, violent punishments for mistakes, or extreme training regimes leading to physical and emotional exhaustion. Such incidents can significantly impact a child star's growth, causing them to live in perpetual fear and apprehension.

It is high time to shift the industry's focus from power and profit to fostering a safe and conducive environment for children. The urgency to address these concerns cannot be overstated. Every child star's potential could dwindle before our eyes if they continue to grapple with abuse hidden behind the coveted sparkle of stardom.

These grim tales of abuse should be seen not just as stories but as a desperate call for intervention. A powerful crusade needs to be launched to restructure Hollywood's machinery, aimed at rooting out these deep-seated exploitative practices. It's time these kids are treated as more than mere commodities and are allowed to enjoy their childhood just as a child should.

Lastly, we must recognize that these are not just horror stories whispered in the dark corners of casting offices, but the genuine experiences of young professionals. It's paramount that the focus moves to prevent such incidents and ensure enough safeguards are in place. It should be everyone's mission to make sure that disillusionment doesn't strangle the dreams of young stars just on the brink of finding their light.

In the end, no one should have to pay such a steep price for their dreams. After all, the dream of being a star should be worth living but not at the expense of mental peace, safety, and basic human rights. For a star to truly shine, it should be allowed to grow, learn, stumble, and rise again, free from the shadows of abuse and manipulation.

For these child celebrities to survive and thrive in the spotlight, it is essential to pull back the curtain on the dark corners of Hollywood's industry and expose these abusive realities. It's time to act, so no child has to pay the dark and painful price for fame.

Abuse Hidden Behind the Glam Shine enthralls as it unearths the dark undercurrents often subsumed by the razzle-dazzle of fame. When rose-tinted views of stardom are stripped away, a more pervasive and ominous reality often surfaces. For many tender-aged stars, the shiny veneer of Hollywood becomes a damning facade, hiding grim tales of exploitation and abuse.

The cheerful smiles, glamorous outfits, and public adoration often act as cosmetic covers concealing grave instances of ill-treatment. This abuse often takes various forms – physical, emotional, or mental, oft aggravated by the immense pressure and glaring exposure that come with fame. In some more sinister cases, the child celebrities are insidiously manipulated by unscrupulous industry persons and even heartbreakingly, their own kin, who exploit their innocence and vulnerability, gorging on primarily financial motives. Having the child's trust exploited is a harrowing ordeals they suffer, sadly behind the glamourous curtain of the showbiz.

Another debilitating fallout of this abusive environment is the hindrance it imposes on the child's emotional and psychological growth. Deprived of healthy emotional outlets, these youngsters resort to turbulent coping mechanisms including rebellion and public outbursts, casting long, bitter shadows on their formative years. It's high time the industry and society collectively acknowledge these hidden scars in the dreams woven with stardust, and endeavor resolutely to prevent such reprehensible exploitation of the innocence and talent of young stars.

Power Play: How Systemic Abuse Affects Child Celebrities

The glamour and dazzle of Hollywood often masks a stark and sinister reality. Child celebrities, propelled into fame and fortune while still innately vulnerable as kids, often fall victims to the grotesque power play that marks the darker corners of stardom. To delve deeper into this, it's crucial to understand the dynamics of power and manipulation within the Hollywood system.

Child celebrities, with potential success and profit attached to their innocent and impressionable identities, often catalyze a warped power dynamic. The constant burden to perform and fulfil expectations bestowed by management, studios, and even the audience, places these young stars in a dangerously stressful and manipulative environment.

This environment often becomes a breeding ground for systemic abuse. Employers, advisors or even parents may resort to coercive tactics to ensure the child's compliance to demands. This can range from verbal intimidation, emotional manipulation, to instances of physical and sometimes, horrifically, even sexual abuse. These kids, while handled with kit gloves in the public eye, can often face deep-rooted and long-lasting abuse behind closed doors.

Steeped in this punitive culture of fear and control, these child celebrities are conditioned to view such abuse as a norm, an inherent part of their career path towards success. They're made to believe that they shoulder the livelihoods of many - their managers, publicists, crews on set, and even their own families. This gross distortion of power not only robs them of a normal childhood but can pave the way for psychological damage that extends well into adulthood.

This systemic abuse often becomes a catalyst for a range of problems. Some can develop anxiety disorders, depression, and post-traumatic stress disorders. Others may resort to substance abuse for escapism or to live up to the 'rock and roll' persona the industry sometimes glorifies. Unsurprisingly, such victims are also prone to public outbursts, rebellious behaviors, and a noticeable struggle with autonomy and identity.

Interestingly, this exploitation is often veiled under an 'exchange' of sorts. The perpetrators, armed with their position of power, offer opportunities, exposure, or career-defining roles in return for the victim's silence or complicity. However, such transactions are in reality nothing short of a violation of human rights and child labor laws.

Moreover, this culture of silence further fuels this cyclical pattern of abuse. Many young stars might not even realize that they're being abused due to the clever orchestration of their circumstances. The pain is either numbed under the intoxication of adoration and success or is cleverly justified as part of their 'deal' with fame.

This abuse, though unforgivably pernicious, is unfortunately not an anomaly. Countless child stars have shared their stories, illustrating a systemic pattern of maltreatment that thrives in the underbelly of Hollywood. The mere frequency and similarity of these stories indicate a need for drastic industry reform rather than individual accountability.

Lastly, this prevailing culture of abuse underlines the importance of vigilant, protective forces in a child star's life. Parents, psychologists, law enforcement agencies, and even publicists should prioritize the well-being of these young talents over profitability and fame. They should also initiate conversations about 'abuse', equipping these kids with knowledge and defense mechanisms to identify and counter such situations.

There can't be anything 'systemic' about exploiting vulnerabilities. Hollywood owes its thriving success to these talents, and it's high time that it reciprocates with sincerity and responsibility. This power play obnoxiously belittles the spirit of creativity and art, leaving a vital need for the industry to collectively address this rampant issue. To build an environment conducive to growth, happiness and integrity, systemic abuse must be dismantled - one brave voice at a time.

The Dark Underbelly of Hollywood brings to light a grim reality that underlines the shimmering facade of the entertainment industry, which is rarely portrayed in the media. It's well established that childhood stardom brings with it a flood of attention and opportunities. However, beneath the glitzy premieres and million-dollar smiles, there lurks a shadowy realm, where the curiosity, naivety, and inexperience of young stars often fall prey to manipulation, coercion, and abuse.

The power imbalance within the industry creates a playground for bullies, where the careers of budding talents can be held ransom, or worse still, be traded off under the guise of 'career advancement.' In such a setting, the young stars often feel cornered, with a voice that's barely a whisper against the roar of the industry. Many are forced to shoulder this burden silently, fearing the backlash they might face if they dared to expose the abusers. This tragic undercurrent not only affects their present but can also leave indelible scars on their psychological health, leading to emotional turmoil and outbursts.

Moreover, this dangerous underbelly is far-reaching and deep-rooted, with tentacles spread across the echelons of Hollywood. It's fueled in part by the culture of silence that encases the industry like an impenetrable veil. In a world that thrives on reputation and appeal, those in power often exploit the system while the victims—the child stars—are left to deal with the aftermath. The effects of this exploitation exacerbate their struggle to navigate through stardom, compounding the existing pressures and contributing to the evident dysregulation in behavior witnessed among child celebrities. Thus, in tandem with the lure of fame and glamour, the dark underbelly of

Hollywood paints a haunting picture of the price young celebrities can end up paying, questioning the very foundation of childhood stardom.

A Rise in Activism and Awareness

As hard as it might be to confront, it's crucial to acknowledge the toxic underbelly of what many young stars have to endure. However, it's equally important to note that tides are beginning to turn. The last few years have seen a growing wave of activism and awareness rising against the inappropriate power dynamics and systemic abuse within the Hollywood industry.

Various elements have contributed to this. The vast reach of social media platforms and the internet has provided a venue for victims to share their stories, helping to shed light and promote conversation around this often veiled issue. This new avenue for expression and solidarity enables young stars, as well as adults, to share their experiences without the fear of immediate retaliation that a more direct confrontation might bring.

Next, the gains made by the #MeToo movement and Times Up's discussion about sexual harassment in Hollywood can't be overstated. The powerful global wave of solidarity marked the start of a significant shift in Hollywood; it created an open space for individuals to voice their grievances and allowed for the public support of victims. Suddenly, the fear of speaking out began to ebb as abusers in power were held accountable.

Furthermore, survivors and allies alike have been pushing for more stringent legislation to protect the rights and mental health of child performers. Laws like the Coogan Law, which protects a certain percentage of a child actor's earnings, have expanded in response, giving these budding performers more control over their destinities.

Simultaneously, an increased emphasis on mental health awareness has played a crucial role in addressing the psychological impact of fame on child stars. With the stigma around mental health issues gradually diminishing, it has led to more public discussions around mental health. Major celebrities have begun openly addressing their struggles, leading to a climate where it's not only acceptable, but encouraged, to seek help.

Non-profit organizations are also stepping in to fill a crucial supportive role. Groups like the Actors Fund, SAG-AFTRA and others offer resources and programs designed to support child actors and their families, helping them navigate the complexities of the industry. From counseling to financial aid, these organizations serve as critical lifelines for young performers and their loved ones.

It's worth mentioning the increased role that Hollywood parents are now playing in the wake of this uprising. Many parents in the industry, who were once part of the problem, are now becoming part of the solution. They are demanding more appropriate working conditions, challenging exploitative contracts, and advocating for the rights of their child-stars with increased fierceness.

Lastly, but certainly not least, the rise of diverse representation and inclusion in the entertainment industry has led to a broader spectrum of stories being shared. As the voices and narratives of previously silenced groups gain prominence, it's becoming harder for the systemic abuse and power misbalances to stay concealed.

While the fight is far from over, the increased activism and awareness are indeed promising developments. This awareness can potentially lead to substantial change in the industry, protecting future child stars from the abuse and manipulations that their predecessors had to endure. On this front, the future looks a little brighter for the young celebrities.

With the walls of silence now crumbling, one thing becomes clear: Hollywood is no longer a place where abusive power can hide unchecked. The new wave of awareness has taken root, and industry change isn't just possible, it's inevitable.

Chapter 7:
Psychological Support for Child Stars

Continuing our exploration into the fascinating and often tumultuous world of child celebrities, we now delve into the ways psychological support can play a crucial role in their lives. When contemplating about childhood stardom, one can't overlook the essential role of a solid support system. It's not just the glitz and glamour but a metaphorical safety net that cushions the tumultuous ride, stemming from the limelight. Too often, young stars are thrust into a world filled with pressure, expectation, and emotional strain, resulting in a whirlwind of mental challenges. The remedy to this is encouraging young celebrities to embrace therapy, breaking down the stigma often associated with these useful interventions. Therapy can act as a lighthouse amidst churning seas, an avenue for relief, understanding, and practical tools to handle their unique circumstances. Becoming a child star doesn't come with an instruction manual, but with therapeutic support, these young talents are provided a compass, guiding them through both the incredible highs and disheartening lows. Additionally, the industry filled with celebrity stories, hints at the instrumental role of therapy in their redemption, providing a mirror reflecting their journey from loss to triumph. Voices that echo survival demonstrate resilience, tangible proof that with the right support, surviving the Hollywood machine is indeed more than just a pipe dream. This narrative through therapy isn't just about surviving but thriving amidst the often chaotic world of fame and fortune.

The Importance of a Support System

There's no denying it. Childhood fame is a thrilling yet treacherous tightrope walk. That said, a robust support system can play an invaluable role in maintaining the mental and emotional health of a young star. Think of it as a safety net ready to catch them when they stumble or fall—contributing not only to their survival but also their sanity amidst the spotlight's glare.

An essential pillar of this support system is, without doubt, the family. Families act as a vital grounding force. In the throes of chaotic schedules and incessant paparazzi, families provide a sense of normalcy and stability. They serve as reminders that, beyond the fame and fortune, these young celebrities are still kids who need love, guidance, and discipline—much like any non-famous child.

However, it ain't all about blood ties. Friends—real, honest-to-goodness friends—add another layer to this support system. It's important for child stars to have friendships with those who treat them as equals, not as commodities or ticket to limelight. These friendships often provide a sense of normalcy, a chance to be simply 'children' and not 'child celebrities'.

Moreover, professionals such as therapists, counsellors, and life coaches often form yet another crucial part of this system. They provide necessary mental health support—guiding young stars through the emotional turbulence that often accompanies fame. This support helps these children process their experiences in a healthy way, equipping them with coping mechanisms that go a long way in preventing public outbursts, mental breakdowns, or even a full-blown career crash.

Mentors within the industry are also quite crucial. These can be older, more seasoned celebrities who have walked in their shoes and successfully navigated the challenges of early fame. They can offer wise counsel borne out of personal experience and save these young ones from learning some lessons the hard way.

The tragic tales of child stars falling prey to the industry are numerous. But so too are the success stories of those who've thrived despite the odds. And the difference often boils down to the strength and quality of their support network. It's the close-knit and caring circle of individuals around a child star that can make a profound difference between a crash-and-burn scenario and a soaring success story.

The entertainment industry must, therefore, prioritize the institution of reliable support systems around these young talents. Instead of solely focusing on quick gains, stakeholders should invest in the wellbeing of these children. After all, in the long term, well-adjusted, happy stars make fewer tabloid headlines, contribute positively to the industry's reputation, and continue generating profit as they transition into successful adult celebrities.

Recognizing the importance of a solid support system is only the first step. Establishing such a system involves continuous effort, vigilance, and resources. Open lines of communication, regular mental health check-ins, and ensuring a well-rounded life outside of work are some of the strategies that go a long way in establishing this safety net.

Child celebrities are, at the end of the day, children who've been catapulted into a world of adult pressures and expectations. A rock-solid safety net of support won't just help them survive; it will allow them to thrive—both as successful artists and as healthy individuals.

The Key Role of a Safety Net cannot be overstated in the success and mental well-being of young celebrities. A carefully woven safety net composed of family, friends, mentors and therapists can protect these young stars from the dangers of early fame and public pressure. Navigating fame at such a young age can indeed be treacherous, hence, having a trusted circle offers a buffer, refilling their confidence and grounding them amidst their stormy ascent.

Just as a trapeze artist wouldn't dare perform without a net below, child stars shouldn't have to either. Many young celebrities are thrust into the adult world at an alarmingly young age, dealing with contracts, shady deals, and ceaseless industry pressure. This abrupt transition often leads them to lose touch with the typical childhood experience, making them feel isolated and misunderstood. A safety net acts as an emotional anchor, providing them respite from these pressures, and allowing them to retain some semblance of normalcy. From supportive parents who protect their interests, to therapists who help them process the complexities of their unique experiences, every contributor to this safety net has a significant role.

Notably, a safety net is more than just a comfortable cushion for a fall - it's preventive as much as it is palliative. It can help young celebrities make wise decisions, encourage them to express their feelings, and assure them that it's okay to take a break from the limelight, emphasizing the importance of self-care. Essentially, such a network serves as their guide and compass in the often maze-like journey of celebrity life, empowering them to navigate fame without losing their grip on reality. Consequently, prioritizing the establishment of this safety net can significantly reduce the risk of damaging behavior and public outbursts, thereby fostering a smoother and healthier transition into adult stardom.

Encouraging Therapy As a Solution More often than not, therapy makes it to the Hollywood scenes featuring a dramatic breakdown or tearful realization. But the movie scenes barely scratch the surface of therapy's potential for supporting child stars navigating their unique pressures. It's high time to pause the silver-screen superficiality and take a closer look at the role of professional mental health support in these young lives.

Imagine what these kids are dealing with- bucket loads of fame, scrutiny under the sparkly microscope of public, and an identity crisis oscillating between their roles on screen and who they truly are. Your typical teen angst pales in comparison, doesn't it? Encouraging therapy for these child stars should not be the exception, but rather the rule, a normalized part of their routine like brushing their teeth or learning their lines. Regular therapy sessions can provide a platform for these youngsters to voice their struggles, doubts, fears, and thoughts without any judgement or fear of public backlash. It can empower them to process fame's complications and learn effective coping mechanisms. And no, therapy isn't just the sign of a meltdown or the precursor of a tabloid headline. It's the silent partner, helping sidestep the possibility of an implosion.

Stigma, bias, or ignorance, whatever be the case, it's about time the Hollywood sphere shook off these inhibitions associated with child stars visiting therapists. The fact of the matter is, therapy provides a safe, confidential space for them to take off their fame garb, be themselves, and heal from the inside out. It's not all about pharmaceuticals or hypnotist watches. Today's therapy techniques run the gamut from cognitive-behavioral strategies to mindfulness practices, all tailor-made for each individual's needs. And let's not forget, it's not just about crisis management. Therapy can also be about prevention, about bulking up emotional immunity, if you please. In the long run, this crucial step can help to neutralize the emotional landmines of stardom, giving these youngsters a fighting chance for a healthier, more balanced adulthood. So, let's chip in to encourage therapy, not just as a solution but a preventive measure. Because fame or not, every child deserves to grow, thrive, and become their best selves.

Celebrity Stories: The Role of Therapy in Redemption

The highest highs and the lowest lows are part and parcel of a child star's arduous journey. But ever so often, there emerges a beacon of hope- a story of redemption, resilience, and positive change. Many times, the unsung hero in these sagas is therapeutic intervention or therapy. It's heartbreaking to see young celebrities spiral downwards and equally inspiring to witness their journey of bouncing back, which often involves therapy.

Therapy, whether it be cognitive behavioral therapy, psychoanalysis, art therapy, or simply talk therapy, has proven to be a lifeline for various celebrities grappling with their private battles while under constant public scrutiny. The role of therapy in the healing process has been substantial, acting as a trusted ally and pivotal support system for these young individuals.

Fame often forces child stars into a lonely existence, isolating them from peers and everyday normalcy. Therapy provides a safe haven for introspection, allowing them to express and explore their feelings in an environment devoid of judgment and intrusion.

Emerging research highlights that narratives of self-understanding and reflection can be vital in promoting resilience. In several documented celebrity stories, it's been observed that therapy has helped frame their adversities within an empowering narrative. It enables them to reinterpret difficult experiences positively, fueling their mental transformation and, ultimately, redemption.

Rehabilitation centers, therapists, and counselors often make use of a multi-pronged approach, combining standard therapy techniques with lifestyle management and coping strategies. This holistic approach has played a significant role in many celebrities reclaiming their lives from the clutches of addiction, depression, or the aftermath of an outburst. Coming through therapy, they're able to reinvent themselves and re-navigate their careers with a refreshed outlook.

While therapy serves as an eminent tool for mitigating the harmful effects of fame at an impressionable age, its role extends far beyond just rectifying maladjustments. Therapy provides the necessary armor for young stars to take on future challenges. It equips them with self-awareness, emotional intelligence, and resilience, qualities necessary to maneuver the labyrinth of the entertainment business.

Protected by the confidentiality that therapy provides, child stars can face and dismantle their buried traumas, a pressing need that is often ignored due to the relentless demand for performances and public personas. These safe spaces mean more than just a place to vent; they become an essential source of personal growth and emotional development.

Several celebrities, post-therapy, have shared their metamorphosis. It's clear from their stories that therapy has a massive role in the restoration of their mental health and the revival of their careers. While fame can erode the innocence and stability of childhood, therapeutic interventions can reconstruct the missing pieces, paving the way for redemption.

In conclusion, tracing numerous celebrity stories clearly indicates that therapy, often misunderstood, derided, or avoided, seems to be a beacon of hope in the tumultuous oceans of childhood fame. Recognizing its role is the first step towards busting the stigma around it and encouraging more young stars to reach out and reclaim their lives.

While we delve further, we should always remind ourselves that fame is multi-faceted, thrilling yet demanding, glamorous yet perilous. But amidst all its complexities, perhaps the simplest truth stands tall; even stars need a helping hand, a shoulder to lean on, and an environment to heal and thrive.

Tales of Triumph: Surviving the Hollywood Machine Where there is darkness, the potential for light is also present. True, fame can be a relentless taskmaster for young stars, meddling with their balanced development, but that's not to say survival, and indeed, triumph is out of reach. Some child celebrities have weathered the storm and emerged triumphant, providing us with invaluable insights into the tangle of fame and its impact on the child star psyche. This sub-section will delve into such tales of victory, as we explore how these young celebrities managed to rise above the challenges of success at an early age.

One cannot deny that the Hollywood machine has a propensity to chew up and spit out many of its young talents, often leaving them in a whirl of mental and emotional turmoil. Yet, we also witness instances where these young stars manage to navigate the treacherous waters of fame. Surviving the Hollywood machine often requires an iron will, a strong support system, and commendably, the ability to remain grounded. Whether it means humbly acknowledging past mistakes and learning from them or managing the external pressures from the industry and the audience, each tale is a testament to resilience and persistence.

Given the intense scrutiny they face, it's not an easy journey and their victories should not be belittled. The 'Hollywood machine' is a relentless beast; to thrive within its jaws, one often needs to harness a power far greater than fame – that of self-awareness. This self-awareness equips our young celebrities with the tools to remain grounded in their sense of self despite the pressures of their environment. In essence, the survival and triumph over the Hollywood machine's pitfalls are a testament to the indomitable human spirit, the ability to persevere through tough times, and ultimately, a testament to the journey of self-growth. While the tales may vary, the common thread of resilience and coming of age is woven through each one. These tales of triumph infuse us with optimism, reminding us that while fame comes with its downsides, survival - and even growth - while in its clutches is possible.

Chapter 8:
The Transition From Child Star to Adult Celebrity

Transitioning from a child star to an adult celebrity can be as tricky as navigating a car on a road full of potholes. As the limelight intensifies, so does the pressure to maintain a spotless reputation and to continually amuse the public's fleeting attention. Growing up inevitably involves stumbling, exploring, and making mistakes - typical rites of passage that become critically examined spectacles when experienced in the public eye. Oftentimes, these young stars can't blend into a crowd or indulge in typical teenage behaviors without repercussion, leaving them feeling alienated or different from their peers. This can ultimately culminate in mental health issues or public outburst as these celebrities struggle to comprehend and navigate their erratic lifestyle and its associated burdens. Coping mechanisms then become a lifeline in the stormy sea of fame, often warranting therapy, reinvention, and a strong support network to ensure a smoother transition into their adulthood. Crafting a new adult persona while staying authentic to oneself is also an indispensable step for these stars, helping them evolve not only in their personal life but also in their professional journey. Successfully transitioning can thus depend greatly on their ability to adapt, cope, and innovate in real-time, their resilience proving crucial in the quest for longevity in a fickle industry.

Growing Up In the Public Eye: The Trials

Decoding the journey of evolving from a child star to an adult celebrity unveils a myriad of trials, a task that only few in the limelight successfully navigate. Transitioning from a child star to an adult celeb doesn't come without growing pains, and oftentimes, these struggles are plastered all over the public forum.

Such figures are known, loved, and scrutinized from a tender age. Their every mistake, every choice becomes instant news fodder. This level of public accountability breeds a unique kind of pressure. It's not just about maintaining an image; it's about balancing one's maturing personal identity with the unwavering glare of an expectant audience.

A precocious child prodigy turned teen sensation isn't given the luxury of normal teenage rebellion. To them, this adolescent rite of passage is marked by public criticism, not by silent understanding. Each controversial stunt, every reckless choice only fuels public discourse about their plummeting 'grace'. Truth be told, it wrecks havoc on their evolving sense of self.

Imagine being caught in the crossfire of blitzing spotlights while trying to carve your niche. You can't just blend into the crowd and find your calling. Instead, your every move is under the radar, magnified for all to dissect. Standing out is both their profession and their curse.

Not to mention, the constant demand to satisfy the audience's insatiable need for entertainment can be stifling. They can't afford to stumble while exploring facets of their true persona that they may want to portray. Graduating from youthful roles to portraying more complex, mature characters is not a cakewalk, as it risks alienating their established fan base.

Privacy is another luxury young celebrities often miss out on. Their relationships, break-ups, friendships, fall-outs, everything becomes the media's business. In no time, the line between their public image and their real self blurs. Continuous scrutiny can spark self-doubt and emotional turmoil, escalating the psychological stress they endure.

In the tangible realm, adjusting to an adult life with financial responsibilities becomes a challenge. Sudden wealth can lead to reckless spending, and the inflow of money might not be as predictable as that of an average salaried individual. Money management, thus, becomes a vital yet daunting chore for these young protagonists of fame.

Total independence blindsides them as they stride into adulthood. While they were previously chaperoned, now they have to make life-altering decisions alone. Surviving the transition might mean rebranding themself, selecting roles that resonate with their personal beliefs yet don't jeopardize their fanbase connection. Quite the tall order, isn't it?

The trials of growing up in the public eye remain an overlooked aspect of fame. Child stars face an uphill climb to establish themselves as mature celebrities, much like a moth metamorphosing into a butterfly. Yet, all we see is the wayward moth or the beautiful butterfly, never acknowledging the arduous process in-between. Truly, it's a journey fraught with struggle, self-exploration, and resilience.

The transition period from child star to adult celebrity is a tightrope, a whirlwind of changes and challenges. It's like a baptism by fire, where stars fortify their mettle and learn to outdo their previous selves. The trials they navigate carve the beautifully flawed, human celebrities we know and admire. Above being a testament to their growth, this journey unravels the raw, human aspect of fame– the tale of a star, just like us, navigating the choppy waters of growing up.

Transitioning Gracefully: Success Stories present a welcome and optimistic turn. If it seems all the talk of mental health crises and public outbursts paints a gloomy picture, we assure you, there's a hopeful side too. Still, that comes with its own set of psychological peculiarities and challenges. But, as you'll see, navigating the choppy waters of fame isn't an impossible task.

Countless child stars have successfully transitioned into accomplished adults, dispelling the notion that early fame is always a catastrophe. Some have leveraged the spotlight to their advantage, enriching their careers and exploring new artistic directions. They're role models not only for future child stars but for anyone weathering the tempest of adolescence and uncertainty. Equally importantly, these success stories paint a picture of resilience, demonstrating that it's possible to overcome even the most challenging situations with proper support, perspective, and perseverance.

As explored in later sections, therapy, robust support systems, and balanced parenting play crucial roles in these success stories. But equally important are self-awareness and internal strength. Every individual's journey is distinct, and what works for one might not work for another. However, commonalities exist, providing a blueprint for others to follow. The insight these stories provide can serve as a guiding light for celebrities embarking on their transitions, and even for onlookers, giving a more comprehensive understanding of what it takes to navigate fame and adolescence with grace and success.

Coping Mechanism: Building a Healthy Adult Celebrity Life

It is a feat in itself to survive the tumultuous journey of childhood stardom and manage to find one's way to adulthood without getting lost in the tunnel of fame. Now the real challenge begins: how to shape up an adult celebrity life that's not only successful but also healthy - emotionally, physically, and psychologically. This is no walk in the park, but the good news is, it's far from impossible. Let's delve into what it takes.

For starters, every celebrity, young or old, needs a strong support system in place that can act as an anchor in the high seas of fame. Friends and family who've always been there can come in handy. They can provide a reality check when needed, ensure that the star doesn't float too far away into the stratosphere of stardom, and keep them grounded. Remember, genuine people who care will tell you what you need to hear, not always what you want to hear.

Next comes the role of personal maintenance. A healthy lifestyle complete with a balanced diet, regular physical exercise, and good sleep hygiene may seem like staple advice for anyone, but it is particularly significant for celebrities. The mental exertion that comes with living in perpetual public scrutiny is intense and can often lead to neglect of the physical self. Prioritizing personal health can, in turn, contribute to mental and emotional wellbeing.

Equally fundamental, if not more so, is the topic of mental health. Regular therapy sessions can help a great deal in navigating the complexities of public life and dealing with the unique rollercoaster of emotions that come with fame. Celebrities are not immune to mental health issues; in fact, they might be more susceptible. Therapy offers a safe space to process experiences and feelings, growth and understanding, and, above all, better coping mechanisms to handle stress and adversity.

As the glare of the spotlight continues, it's important for celebrities to establish some privacy boundaries. Personal life need not be an open-book for the world; boundaries can, and should, be set. Since privacy becomes a luxury with fame, actively carving out personal time and space free from the public eye can act as a healthy retreat and an opportunity for self-rejuvenation.

Another crucial strategy to adult celebrity life relates to career planning. Very often, the transition from childhood to adult roles can be a delicate process. Career reinvention calls for careful choices – selecting roles that challenge while showcasing adult capabilities, yet not alienating the fan base that fell in love with the child persona. This delicate balance is critical for ensuring career longevity and staying relevant in the ruthless world of showbiz.

Learning financial management is also key, considering the heavy paychecks that start coming in early. Having a reliable and trustworthy financial advisor, learning to make impactful, long-term investments, and understanding the value of money can go a long way in ensuring a secure future. It is crucial to remember that fame may be fickle, but financial stability doesn't have to be.

The world of celebrities hosts a rather pernicious phenomenon known as 'impostor syndrome,' where one feels undeserving of the success they've attained. Recognizing this, coming to terms with it, and seeking help if needed are crucial steps towards a healthier adulthood. Accepting that becoming successful at a young age does not make one less deserving of their triumphs is an essential part of the journey.

Building and maintaining a healthy adult celebrity life isn't something that's achieved overnight. It demands continuous work, a whole lot of resilience, and a constant juggling between the public persona and private self. It might seem like walking on a tightrope, but it's certainly achievable with the right mindset and approach.

At the forefront of everything, it is important that the celebrity finds joy in what they do, remains truthful to themselves, and prioritizes personal wellbeing above all. After all, fame without wellbeing is like a shiny gold ring without a diamond – it might draw eyes, but it lacks the sparkle that truly matters.

Navigating the Pitfalls of Transition is an intensive process that can take a heavy psychological toll on young stars, who must grapple with not only the turbulent natural process of adolescence but also the peculiarities of their unique standing in society. Growing up under a microscope and being forced to weather the storms of public scrutiny and personal development simultaneously can be a jolting experience for youth. In the fast-paced world of entertainment where the limelight either makes you or breaks you, the bounce from childhood fame to adulthood celebrity status is replete with hurdles that pose a significant threat to a young star's psychological health.

How can a child star ride the wave of transition without being swallowed up by the magnified challenges? One key to navigating this tumultuous phase lies in leveraging a strong support system. Having a solid circle of family, friends, and professionals who understand the struggles and can offer the necessary emotional, moral, and psychological support is pivotal. Introducing a sense of normalcy into their lives can also counterbalance the overwhelming whirlwind of fame. Simple practices like maintaining a routine, engaging in regular childhood activities, or attending schooling or college can provide the much-needed grounding that buffers against the alienating effects of fame.

Proactively addressing the psychological impacts of transitioning process is equally crucial. This may involve engaging mental health professionals who can offer personalized coping strategies and therapeutic interventions to manage the heightened stress levels and the potential onset of disorders like anxiety or depression. In other words, the journey from a child star to a successful adult celebrity isn't necessarily a steep, uphill battle. With the right mechanisms in place, it can be a navigable path primed with lessons and growth opportunities.

Rebranding: A Crucial Step for Long Term Success

Surviving the early stardom and transitioning into a successful adult celebrity is a complex process, much like navigating an obstacle course while blindfolded. A pivotal, yet often overlooked step in this process is rebranding. This involves more than just updating a wardrobe or changing a hairstyle. Rebranding is a carefully executed strategy to project a new, mature image that aligns with the star's personal growth.

Keeping in mind the psychological complexities that child stars face, rebranding often serves as a cathartic process. It allows them to shed the weight of their childhood fame, break free from preconceived notions, and reinvent their persona on their terms. This not only provides a liberating sense of control but also paves the way for their future success by drawing a clear demarcation between their past and future.

However, successful rebranding is not a spontaneous decision, it's a meticulously planned journey. It requires an acute sense of self-awareness and a clear vision for the future. It also demands resilience, as the process often entails vigorously fending off resistance from those who prefer the child star image to linger.

While the public eye is perpetually keen to critique any drastic changes, the challenge lies in maintaining authenticity. Straying too far from one's authentic self for the sake of rebranding can lead to psychological strain and public backlash. Thus, striking a balance between a new, mature persona and personal authenticity is critical.

Rebranding is not an isolated endeavor. It's integrally linked to developing healthy coping mechanisms and resilience, which are crucial for surviving the industry's pressure cooker environment. The emotional fortitude gained through this process can also prove instrumental in avoiding public outbursts, making rebranding a key to maintaining mental health.

Successful rebranding can have a transformative effect beyond reputation and image. It can boost the celebrity's confidence and arm them with the tools required to navigate the complexities of adult fame. It creates a foundational anchor, enabling them to withstand public scrutiny, criticism, or backlash that inevitably parts of their journey.

Professional resources such as therapists, public relations specialists, and industry mentors are invaluable during the rebranding process. Therapists can offer psychological support during this daunting transition, while public relations professionals can guide the star in making strategic decisions that align with their rebranding goals. Industry mentors, on the other hand, can provide support and insights based on their experience.

However, parental role remains paramount. A supportive and understanding approach from parents can not only cushion the emotional upheavals of rebranding but can also go a long way in lending credibility to the rebranded image. Parents serve as a crucial link between the child's past and future, supporting them through their metamorphosis.

To sum, successful transition from a child star to an adult celebrity invariably requires a strategic rebranding. Coupled with robust psychological support, informed parenting, and a certain degree of resilience, this can not only ensure a smoother transition but also lay the hallmarks of long-term success.

The Power of Image Makeover is a formidable force in the world of young celebrities. Just as a caterpillar morphs into a butterfly, so too does a child star transition into an adult celebrity. Those who navigate this process successfully often do so through a dynamic image overhaul. While we might admire or ridicule such transformations, the psychological implications of it are far more intriguing than the glitz visible on surface.

Image makeovers are not just about new clothes, different haircut or even a lyrical shift in music. They are profound, integrated changes meant to portray growth, mature identity and artistic evolution. Some may see it as a marketing strategy, but in the lives of young celebrities, it can serve as a psychological lifeline. They use it to distance themselves from past roles, moving out of comfort zone or clichéd expectations. These transformations aid them to cement their place in the volatile showbiz industry as they grow, ensuring that fame isn't fleeting but a lasting force.

Failure to successfully navigate this transformation, however, can have dire consequences. The inability to shed the child-like characters once played and embracing an adult-brimming persona can result in frustration which often manifest as rebellious outbursts. Sometimes, image makeovers are miscued: too drastic, too sudden, or mismatched with the celebrity's brand, causing unintended backlash. So, while image revamping, they must strike a balance. Too much change too fast can be just as damaging as not enough change too slow. Hence, the power of image makeover for child stars is an essential part of their transition. Its influence on their psychological growth and well-being, for good or ill, cannot be overstated.

Conclusion

In conclusion, this book shines a light on the underbelly of youthful celebrity fame, addressing its unfiltered effects on child stars. It becomes clear that the pageantry and prestige of stardom, often idealized, can spawn harrowing complexities that translate into errant behavior and psychological torment. While the public can't help but be entranced by the allure of these young prodigies, the scales fall from our eyes as we delve deeper into the psyche of a child star, whose rebellion often reflects their plea for normalcy. Recognition for this often distorted reality is vital in sparking industry reforms, placing a child's mental health and well-being at the forefront. Needs like proper counseling, resilient support systems, parental guidance, and trauma management stand crucial. As acclaimed faces of our society, it should become our prime responsibility to ensure a safer, healthier environment for these promising children. In short, there's a dire need for a compassionate revolution that shifts focus from the screen's radiance and glamour to the hidden shadows of fame.

Reflecting on the Celebrity World

Take a moment, and drinks in the universe of a child star. It's a world filled with enticing glamour and undeniable challenges, which can make or mar a young psyche. Whether we're audience members in the theater or spectators in the thriving culture of celebrity, these themes are almost impossible to escape. Yet, the careful examination of this world helps us better understand the dynamics at play, their implications, and potential for change.

Child celebrities are catapulted into an unforgiving limelight, far removed from ordinary life situations. The fame denies them the much-needed innocence of childhood, replacing it with the adult responsibilities of managing public scrutiny. This burden prematurely rushes development, often causing ruptures in their psychological building blocks.

Consider the level of rebellion we observe in celebrities. While it's typical for a teenager to push boundaries, we can't ignore how magnified this is for child stars. This amplification is often a domino effect — the earlier the fame, the higher the chances of a public outburst. It goes beyond the normal grounds of rebellion; it evolves into a cry for autonomy, a claim for a life lost to the limelight.

The early fame thrust upon these children places an immense amount of pressure on their developing minds. They trade the playground for the limelight, which inevitably hinders their growth trajectories. The pertinence of this absent normality can't be overemphasized. It underlines how the stress and strain of fame initially seep into their psychology and eventually manifest physically.

Child stars' mental health is a topic that gains increased attention in recent years. It's a dual-edged sword, with the fame exacerbating vulnerabilities while the vulnerability fuels the fame. This interplay creates a whirlpool of suppressed trauma. The trauma, suffocating and silent, festers and occasionally explodes in public outbursts—telling signs of the casualties of Hollywood's spotlight.

The role of the parents in shaping— or warping— these young minds can't be ignored. Parents have a fine line to tread; they decide the trajectory of these young stars. Some work in the best interest of their children, providing a safety net from the harsh reality of fame. Others exploit and overlook the psychological welfare of the children, to their detriment.

Furthermore, the abuse that child stars are prone to is a perilous reflection of fame and power in this industry. Some powerful figures exploit these minors, creating a labyrinth of nightmares behind the curtain of glamour. Yet, a beacon of hope shines as more activism and awareness campaigns rise against this systemic abuse.

The psychological support offered to child celebrities is undeniably crucial. It's high time for the conversation about therapy to move from whispered corridors to spotlighted stages. Shattering the stigma starts with understanding its role in aiding redemption. It equips these young stars with strategies to survive the punishing Hollywood machine.

The transition from a child star to an adult celebrity is yet another challenging hurdle. Some successfully navigate this process, emerging as well-grounded adults. Others stumble and trip, struggling to find their footing on an asymmetrical landscape. Regardless, the power of rebranding demonstrates its potency in sustaining the long-term success of child stars.

Reflecting on the celebrity world unearths layers of complexities hidden beneath the star-studded surface. The journey traverses the wide arc of precocious fame to the rugged terrain of adulthood within public scrutiny. It's a telling testament of what happens when we prematurely thrust kids into the limelight that demands more than they can handle.

Despite the seemingly grim portrayal, it isn't doom and gloom. In the darkness, stars are born, and with careful guidance, therapy and supportive networks, these child stars can navigate an era of fame with their sanity intact. It's a tough call, yet certainly not an impossible feat.

Note that the reflection on the celebrity world isn't a call for pity nor a derision of the world of fame. Rather, it's a demand for change—a change in industry practices, child protection laws, parenting, and in our attitudes as spectators. After all, aren't these stars, in essence, children first? Let's not forget to place the child before the fame.

We look forward to a time where the Hollywood machine treats child actors not merely as moneymakers but as individuals with their unique vulnerabilities and strengths. Here's to a future where the psychological welfare of child stars isn't an afterthought, but rather, a priority. Shine on, little lights, may your brilliance illuminate your paths, rather than consume you.

Steps for Industry Change As we've unraveled the complex world of child stardom and the often heartbreaking consequences it can bring, it's crucial to focus our attention towards the changes that need to be implemented within the industry. Remember, the objective here isn't to strip a child off their chance at stardom but rather to ensure their journey in the limelight is guided by healthy measures, irrespective of their unparalleled life.

The first and the most fundamental step towards this change is stringent regulations. Child labor laws exist, yes, but they tend to be lax when it comes to the entertainment industry. We need regulations that strike an equilibrium between work commitments and the psychological needs of a child celebrity. How about mandatory on-set psychologists? Sharing the spotlight between mental health experts and directors can create an environment conducive to both talent and wellness.

Secondly, having a zero-tolerance policy towards abuse - emotional, physical, or sexual, must be set in stone. The industry must ensure that predatory behavior is addressed immediately and with utmost seriousness. This can not only help in assuring the parents about their child's safety but also instilling confidence in the young performers.

Additionally, education should be made mandatory. Let's get it right, there's no profession out there that doesn't require basic education except perhaps in this industry. Home or private tutoring can provide these young talents with an ordinary life experience, simultaneously preparing them for plan B just in case fame doesn't work out for them in the long run.

Lastly, therapy and psychological support should be actively promoted, normalized, and provided. The erratic schedules, overexposure, and scrutiny that these children face can take a toll on their mental health. Facilitating easy access to mental health professionals can go a long way in ensuring that fame doesn't become a burden on their tender shoulders. We must remember, they aren't just stars, they're kids too. And every kid deserves a chance to grow and mature at a pace that suits them best, lights, camera, and action notwithstanding.

Looking Beyond the Glitz and Glamour of fame reveals a lurking shadow that often goes unnoticed - the psychological impact on young celebrities. The world often focuses on the exciting, luxurious life they may lead, with attention poured onto them, movies premiering worldwide, or chart-topping albums. However, amidst these twinkling spotlights and the loud applause, one cannot overlook the toll it takes on these young minds, who are still trying to figure out their identity amid growing up in the public eye.

The reality of fame is more than the glitzy Photoshop pictures we see, it's a constant pressure cooker situation. These bright, talented, and determined young stars are thrust into a world of relentless scrutiny, criticism, and unrealistic expectations at an age when most of their peers are navigating school exams or dealing with first loves. Their life, their growth, their mistakes are under the microscope, and every move could potentially make or break their careers. They often find themselves torn between maintaining a 'picture-perfect' image and wanting to live a normal childhood, a tug-of-war that exerts immense stress and propulsion towards rebellion.

Albeit, fame is not a universal recipe for disaster. Some child celebrities grow up to be well-adjusted adults with a healthy sense of self because they have had the right kind of support system, be it empathetic parents or guardians, or access to therapy and mental health care. However, such instances are exceptions rather than the norm. It's crucial as a society for us to set aside our curiosity, step back from our voyeuristic tendencies, and create room for these young individuals to grow and make mistakes without harsh judgement. When it comes to young celebrities, just looking beyond the glitz and glamour could make a world of difference.

www.ingramcontent.com/pod-product-compliance
Lightning Source LLC
Chambersburg PA
CBHW031322060726
47590CB00003B/1308